"Sunshine" SPC Donald L. Wheeler, Jr. Life of an Infantryman
by Mary Catherine Thorrez-Wheeler

ISBN: 978-0-9888611-0-7

Printed in the United States of America

Sales inquiries:
maryctw@gmail.com

A prayer/poem my children grew up saying
to our Blessed Mother Mary:

"LOVELY LADY DRESSED IN BLUE"

Lovely Lady dressed in blue----
teach me how to pray!
God was just Your little Boy,
Tell me what to say!

Did You lift Him up, sometimes,
Gently on Your knee?
Did You sing to Him the way
Mother does to me?

Did You hold His Hand at night?
Did You ever try
Telling stories of the world?
O! And did He cry?

Do You really think He cares
If I tell Him things----
Little things that happen? And
Do the Angels' wings
Make a noise? And can He hear
Me if I speak low? *(whispering)*
Does he understand me now?
Tell me----for You know.

Lovely Lady dressed in blue----
Teach me how to pray!
God was just Your little Boy,
And You know The Way.

By Mary Dixon Thayer
Popularized by Archbishop Fulton Sheen

Table of Contents

Acknowledgments... i

Introduction.. ii

Prologue: <u>Jacinta the Flower of Fatima</u>............... iii

    1st Prayer taught by the Angel............................ iii

    2nd Prayer taught by the Angel.......................... iv

    Prayer:"Total Consecration to

    Jesus through Mary"... v

Chapter One: The Early Years... 1

    Prayer: "Saint Michael the Archangel"......................... 6

Chapter Two: The Army Years... 8

    Infantry Blue and Our Lady of Fatima Blue Army........ 11

    DJ Raising The Flag... 14

    Our Lady of Charity... 20

    Prayer: "Guardian Angel"... 30

Chapter Three: Iraq Months... 32

    1LT Osbaldo Orozco... 34

Chapter Four: October 13, 2003.. 45

    How to pray the "Divine Mercy Chaplet"..................... 54

Chapter Five: "...Though I Walk Through The Valley..." 56

Chapter Six: Laying to Rest.. 69

    Father Nenneau's Homily... 70

    DJ's Sister's Poem... 73

    DJ's Mom's Reflections... 74

    "Your Cross" by St Francis de Sales 82

    Song "Trust His Heart" by Babbie Mason.................... 83

Tribute by CPL William Velez............................... 87

Memorial to SPC James Powell............................... 90

Chapter Seven: When Darkness Falls Follow The Star............ 94

DJ and Our Lady of All Nations................................100

DJ's Statue of Saint Michael................................103

Chapter Eight: Remembering................................104

Rich man and Lazarus Parable................................106

Teenager's Faith Strengthened................................110

July 15, 2004 DJ's 23rd Birthday........................118

DJ's Memorial Cards................................119

Chapter Nine: God's Mighty Hand 122

Vatican II: Constitution of the Church...........................122

Tribute: The Monument at Withington Park
    in Jackson, Michigan................................134

Tribute: SGT Donald L Wheeler, Uncle Don................137

DJ's Michaels................................140

Chapter Ten: Religious Understanding of The
    Ultimate Sacrifice...........................141

Sr. Lucia's Vision of Trinity Cross................................141

How to Pray The Rosary................................142

The Lessons Learned From Being DJ's Mom.............. 145

Author's Background................................147

"...the little child will lead them..." Isaiah 11:6-9................148

ACKNOWLEDGMENTS

"I, Mary Catherine Thorrez-Wheeler, humbly present this Good Work to You, O Lord, but I fear that the stain of self-love that often accompanies my gifts will cause You to reject it.
So I petition You, my dear Mother, Blessed Mary, Queen of Heaven and earth, to accept this Work in Your most agreeable and worthy Hands for God will not consider so much the thing that is given to Him as the Mother Who presents it."
(Saint Louis de Montfort, True Devotion to the Blessed Virgin Mary page 107-109)
Grant this through Jesus Christ, Your Son, Who lives and reigns with You and the Holy Spirit, one God, for ever and ever. Amen.

THANK YOU, to my sons,
BURT, THOMAS, QUENTIN and PAUL.
Your knowledge, support, and more importantly your love meant everything.

THANK YOU, TRACY NUNLEY for being a good friend.
Our mutual Trust in our Lord Jesus brought us together
and your assistance fortified me on this journey.

MILITARY/VETERANS are people who at one point in their life wrote a blank check made payable to the

UNITED STATES OF AMERICA

for an amount of up to and including their life.
ALL AMERICA SAYS, *"THANK YOU!"*
My personal Thank You to DJ, Quentin, Paul, Spencer, Dominic, and Patrick Wheeler...my sons.

MAY THE MESSAGE OF OUR LADY OF FATIMA BE LIVED:

1. PRAYER especially the rosary to obtain the Grace to perform duties in life properly and for peace in families and the world.
2. PENANCE means to turn away from sin and turn back to God and make reparation for sinners.
3. DEVOTION to the Immaculate Heart of Mary.

i

INTRODUCTION

It is May 24, 2012. I stand for the Gospel of the Seventh Week of Easter as a pre-postulant in a Visitation Monastery. The 17th Chapter of Saint John is being read for the third and final day. In this chapter Jesus is reminding His Father of Their private Words before His Mission began on earth. It is The Son's last request before beginning His Passion. Each day I had been taken into this tender scene in a personal way due to the fact that I am a parent. I could visualize how the Father's Heart must have melted upon hearing His Only Begotten Son's prayer before He gives The Ultimate Sacrifice. As a Loving Father I could see Him look at His Son and say, *"Anything for You, Son."* My thoughts were interrupted with the words, *"And you?"*

To understand those Words, I was lead to recall a wedding and DJ was the best man. The only problem was he could not be there because he was in lock-down at his base since he was soon to be deployed into Iraq. So when it was the time for toasting the bride and groom, with no best man present, I spoke in his stead, though it was not planned. Later that night when we talked he was crying,

*"Thanks, Mom, for **speaking for me**. I couldn't have done as good of a job as you did."*

"Oh, baloney, DJ. You are a good speaker and when you get home we all will be listening, just waiting to hear what you will have to say."

SPC Donald L. Wheeler, Jr.'s voice was silenced on October 13, 2003. In eulogizing my son, I spoke these words:

**"...It will be my commitment to DJ to help his message
to our family be shared with the world...."**

The *"And you?"* was God reminding me to honor my commitment to my son?

**THOSE WITH EYES... SEE
THOSE WITH EARS... *"LISTEN"***

PROLOGUE

To begin to tell the story of my son, DJ, I must write first about an event that happened back in 1916-1917. In fact it was not just *one* event, but two events that led to a real awakening for the town of Fatima, in the country of Portugal, and then to the world. The events happened because the hearts of three children were open. They were already obedient to their parents and going to Mass and in the habit of working and praying together. They were fertile ground for the Word of God to be planted so His Grace could grow to complete His Work. The first event was a series of three encounters with the Angel of Peace. In Jacinta the Flower of Fatima by Rev. Joseph Galamba de Oliveira, Sister Maria Lucia de Jesus, the eldest of the children, describes these encounters.

"The time seems to have been between *April and October* of 1916 the angel appeared to us… it began to drizzle...We looked for a cliff to use for a shelter...we spent the day... ate our lunch and said the rosary... when a strong wind shook the trees... We began to see... the form of a transparent youth more brilliant than crystal transfixed by the rays of the sun... he said, *'Do not fear. I am the Angel of Peace. Pray with me.'* And kneeling, he bowed his head to the ground...

"My God, I believe, I adore, I hope, and I love you.
I ask you for pardon for those who do not believe, who do not adore,
who do not pray, who do not love you."

After repeating this three times, he arose and said, *'Pray thus. The Hearts of Jesus and Mary are attentive to the voice of your supplication.'*... The second Apparition...midsummer... Suddenly, we saw the same Angel near us. *'What are you doing? Pray, pray much. The Hearts of Jesus and Mary have designs of Mercy upon you. Offer prayers and sacrifices constantly to the Almighty.' 'How are we to sacrifice ourselves?'* I questioned. *'In everything you can, offer a sacrifice as an act of reparation for the sins by which He is offended, and of supplication for the conversion of sinners. Thus draw peace upon our country. I am its Guardian Angel... Above all, accept and endure with submission the suffering which Our Lord will send you.'* These words were engraved on our hearts like a light, which made us understand Who God was, how He loved us and wanted to be loved, and the value of sacrifice, how pleasing it was to Him, and how because of it He converted sinners... From that moment on we began to offer to our Lord everything...The third time...he appeared...carrying in his hand a Chalice and above it a Host from which a few Drops of Blood fell into the Chalice. Leaving the Chalice and the Host suspended in mid-air, he prostrated himself on the earth, and repeated three times:

"MOST HOLY TRINITY, Father, Son, and Holy Spirit,
I adore Thee profoundly. I offer Thee the Most Precious Body, Blood,
Soul, and Divinity of Jesus Christ present in all the Tabernacles
of the world, in reparation for the outrages, sacrileges, and indifference
by which He is offended. And through the infinite merit of
His Most Sacred Heart and the Immaculate Heart of Mary,
I beg of Thee the conversion of poor sinners."

Then raising himself, he...gave me the Host, and the contents of the Chalice to Jacinta and Francisco, saying... *'Eat and drink the Body and Blood of Jesus Christ, horribly outraged by ungrateful men. Make reparation for their crimes, and console your God.'* He prostrated himself on the ground and... with us repeated the...Most Holy Trinity prayer and then disappeared"(pgs. 78-82).

The Angel of Peace has another name, Saint Michael, the Archangel; which is verified in the Liturgy of the Hours on the Feast of the Archangels, September 29. Saint Michael and his angels restored peace in Heaven by banishing the bad angels. What warrants one to be called "bad"? Anyone who chooses their own will over God's. This heavenly Warrior came to the children as Teacher, not to teach physical combat but to teach spiritual combat through prayer, thus preparing the way for Blessed Mary and through Her Immaculate Heart true peace will reign.

The second event was a series of six apparitions of Blessed Mary; Mother of God, Queen of Peace and Queen of the Rosary; which began on May 13, 1917 and on the thirteenth for the next five months. She came to enforce the importance of praying by saying,

"Pray. Pray constantly, and make sacrifices for many souls go to hell because there are none to mortify themselves and to pray for them"(pg 104).
"The Lady... again urged the recitation of the rosary as a means of bringing the war to an end"(pg 19). *"... the Lady had announced...they must sacrifice themselves for sinners"*(pg 99).
"Our Lady,(spoke)...with kindness and sadness:...'God wishes to establish in the world the devotion to My Immaculate Heart. If they do... many souls will

be saved and there will be peace. This war will end...in the end my Immaculate Heart will triumph...and some time of peace will be granted to the world'''(pg 119-120). A miracle was promised for October 13, 1917, *"to testify to the truth of the apparitions and the authenticity of the message"(pg 29).* This Day is referred to as The Miracle of the Sun when, *"Suddenly the sun trembled as though shaken by a giant hand,...began to spin...like a wheel of fire,...projected...multicolored rays of light"(pg 31). "detach itself... careening toward the earth"(pg 33).* 70,000 people witnessed this display and thought it was the end of the world but soon realized that their fear of God had been replaced by *"a rebirth of faith, confidence and love in each deeply stirred soul"(pg 34).*

You may be asking yourself why did Blessed Mary choose shepherd children? Father John A. Gallas from the website **Courageous Priest** addresses this question.

"The fact that Blessed Mary chose shepherd children of simple faith is striking. Shepherds were the first to receive the message that Christ was born. Jesus spoke of His relationship with the Church as the "Good Shepherd"*(John 10:1-18, Ps. 23 and 95:7, Ezek 34:11-16, Jer 23:1-6).* Shepherds face personal temptations toward cowardice and laziness, as well as an acute awareness of actual physical dangers (e.g., the attack of wolves). The children understood that God has a flock that is in great danger —unless it is tended, it will go astray. Despite their youth and lay state, they were to **participate in the Church's role of shepherding sinners by virtue of the Grace of their Baptism, and by uniting themselves to the Cross of Jesus Christ through prayer and penance.**"

May we Catholic Christians live out our baptismal promises by receiving the Sacraments often to obtain God's Grace and the Gifts of the Holy Spirit so to strengthen the Mystical Body of Christ, The Church. Please make time to renew your Baptismal Promises through this prayer, **"Total Consecration to Jesus through Mary"**

I, N____, a faithless sinner, renew and ratify today in Your Hands the vows of my baptism. I renounce forever satan; his pomp and works and I give myself entirely to Jesus Christ, the Incarnate Wisdom, to carry my cross after Him all the days of my life, and to be more faithful to Him than I have ever been before. In the presence of all the heavenly Court I choose You, this day for my Mother and Mistress. I deliver and consecrate to You, as Your slave; my body and soul, my goods, both interior and exterior and even the value of all my good actions, past, present and future, leaving to Thee the entire and full right of disposing of me, and all that belongs to me, without exception, according to Thy Good Pleasure, for the greater Glory of God, in time and in eternity. Amen

CHAPTER ONE: THE EARLY YEARS

DJ's life began with a connection to Our Lady of Fatima. During his first trimester, problems developed and it was very important for me to "lay low", which wasn't easy since I was a mother of three, all under the age of three. Adding to my stress, my doctor advised me not to have more than three children. In addition, there was the physical component – memories of the birthing process were as vivid as ever. It terrified me to even think of enduring that pain again! I truly questioned my ability and strength. But I remembered the phrase from my Catholic upbringing:

"When crosses come, God won't give you more than you can handle."

As the pregnancy normalized I made a trip to a Catholic store and ran across the book, *"Jacinta, the little Flower of Fatima"*, which will be my resource for any quotes in this book unless noted otherwise. Blessed Mary would appear saying, *"Do not offend God, our Lord, anymore because He is already grievously offended!"*(pg. 157). She asked, *"Do you wish to offer yourselves to God to endure all the sufferings which He wants to send you, as an act of reparation for the sins by which He is offended and as a supplication for the conversion of sinners?"*(pg 87). Jacinta's response should be ours,

"I do"(pg. 106).

With this new inspiration I was motivated to make whatever sacrifices I could for souls and changed my perspective on life in general and on child-birthing, specifically. It was still going to be painful, but I was no longer afraid. Now the birth of my fourth child had turned into a blessing in every sense of the word, which helped me to embrace the upcoming birth and willingly hand it over to God. The child growing inside of me, DJ, prodded me on to a new level of Faith – Joy in the Cross!

"The wolf shall dwell with the lamb and the leopard shall lie down with the kid, the calf and the lion and the sheep shall abide together and a child shall lead them"(Is 11:6).

IMPORTANT NOTE: There were nine more babies after DJ, total: 13 – my ninth was a miscarriage.

July 15, 1981, my fourth baby was born, Matthew Christopher. Yes, you heard me correctly that was the name my husband would allow. I had asked several times during the beginning months of the pregnancy that if it was a boy could we name him Donald Laverne Wheeler, Jr., because the due date was just a month and a half after Uncle Don's birthday. Uncle Don was an Army Sergeant who died in the Korean War at the age of 23. Without realizing it, we had chosen Uncle Don's birthday as our wedding day. I knew somehow our 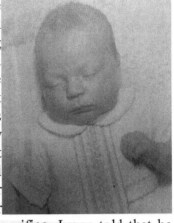 marriage would honor him for his great sacrifice. I was told that he had loved children, but since he never married, he never experienced fatherhood. What better way is there to honor someone! But each time I asked, I was told to think of another name. So when our eight pound, eight ounce baby boy was born I cried out, with great joy, *"Matthew Christopher!"* When I was wheeled into the recovery room and left alone, the still, small, Voice brought back the idea of honoring Uncle Don, but I was fearful to bring up the subject again. Though, when my husband returned, I put aside my fear and asked one last time. This time he agreed! I was so happy for his change of heart and very grateful for the still, small, Voice that gave me the courage to speak. I knew Uncle Don was smiling, too.

"...and after the earthquake a fire, but the Lord was not in the fire; and after the fire a still small voice... Elijah heard it..."(1Kgs 19:12-13).

I taught only one religion class when the kids were very young and it was DJ's fourth grade. One of the topics to be covered that year

was vocations. Now I know most people think a vocation is the call to be a priest or a nun, but I believe that God wants whatever job we do to bring Christ to the world. I was going to have the class make a poster depicting, with magazine pictures or drawings, all the different jobs that had their interest. I needed a title for this poster, other than the obvious. God revealed it to me during Mass, Philippians 2:15-16,
  "Shine on the world like bright stars, you are offering it the Word of Life."
It was perfect! Once again God knew my need and led me to the answer. That phrase struck me deep in my soul. It changed even the smallest thing that I did into something great because my intent was for God's Glory! *Lives intertwined strengthening both of us. God is so good!*

When I was pregnant with my 13th baby I was looking forward to getting off my feet. The older kids wanted to play outside while the youngest ones took a nap so here was my chance. As I was putting the pillow under my head the still, small Voice asked me where was DJ? I thought he was with the kids outdoors playing 'fort' in the woods but I knew I had better check. After much searching and calling to no avail, I finally called the police. On their way to our house with a search dog they found DJ walking along the main road about seven miles away. His explanation, he wanted to go to Australia because he was interested in their wildlife – the platypus in particular.

A couple months later when I was not able to get to sleep I headed to the family room to watch a little television and do some stretching exercises to relax. After about twenty minutes I headed back to bed. As I turned a corner I saw someone out of the corner of my eye coming into the kitchen. I called out, *"Who's up?"* As I turned to get a better look, I saw a head rise, exposing big eyes and with arms folded in front of the waist, backed up very slowly, went out of view. I thought, "DJ?" only because of the build. I checked every bedroom and everyone was asleep. I never did discover who it was, but because I never felt scared or frightened I believed God gave me a glimpse of a Guardian for our family, letting me know I was not alone. I still feel the lasting effect of peace and love.

February 26, 1995, DJ was confirmed. Confirmation is a Sacrament of the Catholic Church where the Bishop extends his hand over each person, infusing within their souls the Gifts and Fruits of the Holy Spirit. It is at this moment that you are recognized as an adult in the Catholic Church and a Soldier for Christ. A requirement is to pick a saint you look up to and want to emulate and want them to be close to you all your life and intercede for you to God. DJ chose Saint Michael, the Archangel. This Archangel was the one who confronted evil and eliminated it in Heaven. I knew when DJ picked Saint Michael that any battles he would face in life, Good would prevail. The face of this Archangel is not really known, but since Saint Michael means "Who is like God," DJ decided to have the Face of Jesus on his Confirmation stole (a strip of cloth about six inches wide and six feet long, hung evenly around the neck). He asked me to paint it on, as I enjoy painting, and it would be a labor of love since it was a gift for my son. At the rehearsal for this big day, they were told to

wear their finished stoles. Usually, because of his height, DJ would be sent to the back of the group. But because the final call to the Sanctuary was less formal, it did not matter where they stood. I will never forget seeing my son standing front and center, head held high, with the biggest smile. Moments like these are what makes parenting such a sacred job; we get to witness those big moments of change. I knew the Holy Spirit, through His still, small, Voice, inspired DJ to stand front and center and he listened and obeyed. *God is very much involved in all our lives. We just need to take the time to listen, recognize Him in action and praise Him.*

> *"...God loves us, how simple He is, though incomprehensible, and how easy it is to commune with Him, despite His great Majesty"*
> (Diary of Saint Faustina pg 253 #603).

4

In 1999, DJ graduated high school. He had a job that offered him a good future, but his interest turned to the military. A friend had joined and DJ came to me in early summer, 2001, wanting to know what I thought about him signing up. I told him to pray about it before making such a big decision that could change the course of his life. I advised him to seek out people who were more informed and to continue to ask God to guide him. I would be supporting him with my prayers and I trusted God would hear and answer him.

A month or so later, DJ very excitedly approached me about a movie he wanted me to watch and proceeded to connect the DVD player to the television and said,

"Come on, Mom, sit down. You're going to like it."

"All this fuss," I said smiling, *"How can I say no."*

The movie showed a contrast of two men. One man is focused on getting back to his family and his farm after putting in his time as a soldier. He had done such an admirable job, winning the praise and honor of the men who served with him, he was offered a position of wealth, power and prestige. He was not interested. His love for his family and the simple life was all that he desired. The other man had been born into privilege and greedily had his heart set on gaining power and possessions. He soon realized life was not going to work out the way he planned so he manipulated the circumstances. His way meant death and destruction of his own family but that did not stop him. His self-obsession did not allow for love – he only knew fear, which grew to resentment, until it exploded into anger.

There was a line in the movie that struck me and later I saw it on posters under the image of the hero:

"WHAT WE DO IN LIFE ECHOES IN ETERNITY"

I believe what you did with your life, DJ, will continue to echo here on earth as well into eternity. ***All for God's Glory!***

September 11, 2001 – a day many lives changed. Many Americans will never forget where they were and what they were doing as the news unfolded throughout that day. Within days, Donald Laverne Michael Wheeler, Jr. came to me with a decision,

"I am going to join the Army to help fight the evil that has hit our world."

I saw determination in his eyes. This decision was not coming out of an emotional position but from a man on a mission. I was quiet for a few seconds – long enough for me to have a flashback of my little boy running, playing, laughing – eager to experience the world. Now I was looking at a future American Soldier. The word *"evil"* in his statement reminded me of this prayer:

Saint Michael the Archangel, defend us in battle.
Be our protection against the wickedness
and snares of the devil.
May God rebuke him, we humbly pray, and do
thou, O Prince of the heavenly Host,
by the Power of God thrust into hell satan and all
the evil spirits who wander through the world
seeking the ruin of souls. Amen.

I knew this American Soldier would have this heavenly Warrior always watching over him. Coming back to reality I told him,

"I know you have been praying about this and I am positive that God has helped you arrive at your decision and I support it."

As I reached out to hug my son I realized that life as we knew it would be forever changed. We soon would know what it meant to be a military family. A few days later he asked me if I was truly okay with him joining the Army. I reminded him that I had been praying for him since he last spoke to me about joining the military and I felt confident that this was God's Will. *God called through that still, small Voice and DJ listened.* I was indeed very proud of his decision. He informed me that everyone else was against it except for Grandpa (my Pa) and me. He really appreciated my support.

I was deeply aware that his decision could potentially put his life in harm's way. Battles were going on and new ones were developing and I knew DJ could be in the front lines. My mother's heart came to the surface many times but only when I was alone. Yet even then that still, small, Voice would assure me,

"DJ is in My Hands"

so I would dry my eyes and continue in confidence and trust what I *heard* in my heart.

I felt the need to have my extended family to unite in support and prayer as my son began his new mission. I sent out invitations for what I coined "A Blessing Luncheon" for November 3, 2001. The Holy Spirit, through our parish priest with his hands raised over DJ's head, renewed the Gifts of courage, strength, and perseverance. With that, DJ was on his way to boot camp at Fort Benning, Georgia.

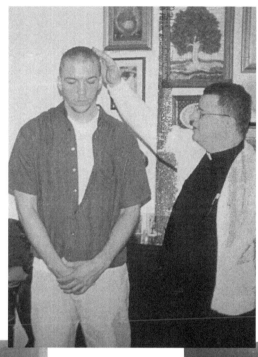

CHAPTER TWO: THE ARMY YEARS

11-18-01   0900 hrs

Hello, everyone. Finally have time to write even though I'm not a big fan of it. I thought I'd tell you how I've been, since it's so hard to get ahold of you on the phone. Been sick for a couple days but I am getting over it finally. Right now I am in Initial Entry Training which is when they issue you all of your clothes and get you in a routine of getting up early and waiting. I received word last night that I leave here and get to go down range, which means I start basic training. But until then all the time I'm spending here doesn't count for anything. They told us also that graduation is on March 22nd, if I can stay healthy. So there is a date to look forward to. There really hasn't been anything exciting happen yet because we don't do anything. So how is everyone? Tell them to write me. This address I'm giving you is temporary, then on the 27th it will change. After I leave this part I'll have more to write about. Well, love you all. See you in December. (DJ was home for Christmas, 2001, and New Year's 2002.) *After I get stamps next week I'll try and write everyone else.*

Love, DJ

LOYALTY: Bear true faith and allegiance to the U.S.
Constitution, the Army, your unit,
and other soldiers.
DUTY: Fulfill your obligations.
RESPECT: Treat people as they should be treated.
SELFLESS-
SERVICE: Put the welfare of the Nation, the Army,
and your subordinates before your own.
HONOR: Live up to all the Army Values.
INTEGRITY: Do what's right; legally, and morally.
PERSONAL
COURAGE: Face fear, danger, or adversity
(physical or moral)

DJ will be wearing a Star!

02 Jan 12   0700 hrs

Howdy, Everyone. It was a little colder than I expected when I got back to base. It was in the 20's. I was a little better adapted to that type of weather being from Michigan but it still wasn't easy. Well, I got to Birmingham (He stayed with a buddy that he met through basic training) *at about 2:30 in the morning which is actually 3:30 because you lose an hour going to Alabama so I got to the hotel at about 4:00 or so and got up at 7:30. I couldn't sleep later it was weird. But we headed out at 11:00 and did some sightseeing and went back to my Company at about 5:00. It's been a*

8

little harder coming back and trying to hold my same standards but I'm getting back to where I was. We ran 4 miles yesterday, that was hard. But we started B.R.M. (Basic Rifle Marksmanship) *this past week and we get to shoot today. I have some time to kill so I thought I'd write you.*

02 Jan 13 0830 hrs

Hey I'm back. (this letter was written on the same paper with the above letter) *It's Sunday and we get to clean the barracks and write letters. I went to the range to shoot yesterday, shot 12 rounds and grouped in 6 which is good. But then it started to rain after I was done which was about 11:30 hrs so I had to wait for everyone else to get done which was about 1700 hrs and it was about 30 degrees. It was fun. Tomorrow I zero in my rifle. My platoon is in the lead by four which is good for us. We get to listen to Nickelback while we clean. They're rock n' roll, Quentin and Thomas know them. I'm feelin' good today. Had nine hours of sleep and slept the whole night to 0600 hrs. which is late. But time is just floating. Love you all. Thanks for the letters, Mom.*

Love, DJ

Oh, send me our Christmas picture and any others like those on my desk with me, Wes, Thomas, Quentin. Thanks.

02 Feb 04

Hi, Mom. How's everything with your leg and all. (It was actually my knee due to a snowmobiling mishap) *Hope you're healing all up. Finally have some time to write. I got pretty sick a couple of weeks ago when the playoffs were happening and they let us watch it on Sunday but I was too sick. I tried calling a week ago but no one answered. Well, since the last time I wrote I have qualified with my M-16 and I got 31 out of 40 which is a sharpshooter. I got my first medal! I have shot a rocket launcher and a grenade launcher. Spent about 5 nights out of the past 7 in the field which is another reason for not being healthy and I shot my M-16 in complete dark with night vision and lasers, all pretty high tech stuff, and tomorrow night we learn night infiltration. It's like laser tag. I've painted my face a couple times and not showered for days. It's been a lot of hard training mixed with fun. I love you all. See you all soon. I really enjoy getting mail. Even though I can't write as often. Sorry it's messy, in a hurry. O yeah, I get to road march Thursday with a 50 pound ruck sack on my back* (an oversized backpack) *and 12 pound rifle in my hand. It's a lot of fun! Mom you need to send more pictures like the others, possibly one with you!* (What mother's heart doesn't melt when her son actually wants a picture of her.) *Talk to you later.*

Love, DJ

March 22, 2002 was graduation from boot camp. DJ's dad and I went down to attend the ceremony. It turned out DJ was having trouble with some of the strengthening test - the Army's P.T. (physical training). His drill sergeant approached us to ask if we could be at his final testing the next day at four in the morning before the formal graduation ceremony. DJ was not too talkative because he was concerned about passing the test .

Now I had a fleeting thought that maybe the Military was *not* where God wanted DJ. Maybe I could take my son back home because of some physical issues. I could live with that. But then I thought of DJ. *Could he?* Probably not. So I put aside my wants and my desires and kept focused on what DJ wanted.

The next morning when the testing began I took to pacing the wet grass several feet away from DJ and began chanting different phrases like: *"You can do it, DJ!" "Do it for your brothers and sisters." "Come on!" "We are so proud of you." "Hang in there!" "Almost done, DJ."* All the while I was visualizing angels around him. When all was said and done, Donald Laverne Wheeler, Jr., was a soldier in the United States Army!

Graduation Day, March 22, 2002
Fort Benning, Georgia

He was told by his drill sergeant to change into his Class A's, (ASU Army green Service Uniform). I grabbed him before he went into his barracks to hug him and congratulate him. He smiled and, hugging me, said he was very relieved that it was over. While he was changing, two of my daughters closest in age to him, one older by sixteen months and one younger by fifteen months, arrived from Tennessee and Ohio, respectively. I was thankful they were there and so was DJ. Then the officer in charge asked me if I would like the honor of pinning the light blue cord designating that my son graduated boot camp, called "Turning Blue Ceremony." Such an honor – of course I would!

Infantry **Blue** and Our Lady of Fatima **Blue** Army. A color was bringing DJ and Blessed Mary together. Since I don't believe in coincidences, I needed to know more.

* The history of the Infantry's Blue goes back to George Washington and the Revolutionary War but officially established in 1904 and then in 1951 during the Korean War, *(connecting DJ and Uncle Don!)* the Army leadership wanted a visual way to encourage the foot soldiers. In using the Infantry Sky Blue Cord, constructed in what is called a Solomon bar, (Solomon, which means 'peacemaker', in the Old Testament: *"...will be a peaceful man and I will give him rest from all enemies on every side... I will bestow peace and tranquility... he will be a son to me and I will be a Father to him"*(1Chr: 22: 9-10).) worn on the right shoulder, became a way to announce to everyone that they would be on the front-lines when our Nation goes to war.

In my research, I also discovered the Infantry is known as the *"Queen of the Battle"*. It gets this title because it does everything and is the most important *piece* in the game of war. Just like in chess the queen is the most important piece because she can move in any direction and take any foe.

* The founder of the Blue Army of Fatima, Father Colgan, had a heart condition and doctors said he would be dead in a few months. He prayed to Our Lady of Fatima and vowed he would spread devotion to Her if She would heal him. Diagnosed completely healed he told his parishioners, *"We will be the Blue Army of Mary and Christ against the red of the world and of satan."*

A blue ribbon or clothing was worn as a reminder of this devotion. Father Colgan sums up Our Lady of Fatima's messages:

1.) Devotion to the Immaculate Heart of Mary.
2.) Pray the rosary daily.

11

3.) Perform your duties in life properly.

May the Infantry title, *"Queen of the Battle"* and their wearing of blue have the *spiritual* intent to honor Blessed Mary, Our Lady of Fatima, the Queen of Peace, to aid their fight against the enemies of our Nation and the evil that prowls about the world seeking the ruin of souls.

Now it was time for the bigger ceremony which meant it was time for us to go to the football field to wait. We enjoyed the day, even with the unusual cold weather because of our pride in DJ's accomplishment. Among all the other presentations, the highlight for me was seeing the Bradley Fighting Vehicle in action. It came out under a cloud of green smoke, then the back dropped down and soldiers came rushing out with their weapons at the ready - very impressive! Then soldiers from all the companies paraded past the bleachers. We were

able to find DJ quite easily because of his tall stature. It was a moment I will never forget. DJ had done what he had set out to do. He was a soldier in the United States Army.

The real beginning of the celebration for me was the pictures afterward. Smiles were contagious! We got to meet many of his friends of which I cannot recall one name – a fact I am sure does not make DJ happy. I'm just horrible with names. Then we went to the

barracks so DJ could change into civilian clothes and get his gear. We could not help him carry anything because he had "orders." The bags were very heavy but he handled them like it was nothing. The effect of his training was being displayed and I was very impressed. All packed, we headed to a restaurant where we could be waited on and relax. Time flew by and before we knew it, it was time for the girls to head north by car and we needed to get to the airport. DJ flew home with us because he had a couple of weeks leave. It made my day just to see him walk in the house and hear him say,

"Hey, Mom."

His new base was Fort Hood, Texas. This was the same one my Pa had been stationed in during 1944, before being sent to the Philippines during WWII to stop the invading Japanese. DJ said,

"If it was good enough for Grandpa, it is good enough for me."

I had my annual Easter breakfast at the house for many family members. When it was over and people began to leave, suddenly my Pa asked DJ to put on his uniform. The results for complying with that request are the most treasured pictures I have of my son, the soldier. My Pa checked him over, respecting the fact that his grandson was in a United States Army Class A green Service Uniform (ASU). I know DJ was happy that he had something in common with his Grandpa – the Army. The smile on DJ's face will be forever embedded in my mind. For that I have my Pa to thank. I like to believe he was listening to that still, small, Voice, because he was usually the first person to want to leave a party. *Thank you, Pa, for listening.*

The damage done to my knee because of snowmobiling did require an operation, soon after he left in April. I recuperated well enough for me to receive the doctor's permission to drive twenty hours with four of my children to Texas to see DJ for an early 21st birthday. I had not missed one of his birthdays and I did not want to start. We celebrated it in June because he was in training during his actual birth date, July 15. He did not have much time to be with us so we used the time to shop for birthday presents. After the purchases we wrapped everything from shoes, to cakes, to balloons. Then we put the gifts into a bigger box and wrapped it, too! We told him he was not

13

allowed to open the presents until his birthday, with one exception. I had found a four inch statue of Saint Michael the Archangel, his Confirmation Saint. It was the only present I saw him unwrap! I was reminding DJ and Saint Michael of their commitment to each other and asking Saint Michael to continue to guide and protect my son. I felt very confident God allowed him to hear my prayer.

While we were there DJ had been given the duty of raising the American Flag in the morning and lowering it in the evening. This would be the first action I would witness my son perform as an American Soldier. I would not miss it and will never forget it for as long as I live. I shared this when I was asked to speak at the **"Fallen Heroes Memorial Concert"**organized and performed by Kelly Trudell (http://www.kellytrudell.net/) and Company to honor DJ, Matthew Soper, Brent Beeler, and James Collins, Jr. on March 6, 2010.

"The first morning I woke the kids up so we could witness DJ fulfilling part of his duties as an American Soldier. The grass was still wet as we hurried to get into position, spreading ourselves around the area of the flag pole. And then out from Building One three soldiers in Battle Dress Uniform (BDU's) came marching in single file. DJ was leading – easy to spot since he was 6'4" tall. The quiet of the morning was now broken by the sound of their boots hitting the pavement, marching in unison. The last one in the line stopped at a certain point but kept his feet moving. DJ and the middle soldier continued on toward the flag pole. Once at the pole it was quiet again. DJ was responsible for the rope and hooking the Flag to it while the second soldier kept the Flag from touching the ground. DJ worked with smoothness, precision, and focus until finally the Flag unfurled and headed for the heavens. With tears flowing, taking pictures proved to be a challenge. I cried because this scene felt sacred with the Sun coming up darkness. It was Our soldiers were darkness of evil so of Freedom into the familiar red, waving, alerting United States of Nation under honored to have ceremony, a continues on every morning and every Afterward DJ told called into the office who said in  piercing the very symbolic. fighting the to bring the Light the world. Seeing white, and blue all that this is the America – a proud GOD. I was witnessed this ceremony that base every evening. us they had been Post Commander's all his years being in the military, twenty-some-odd years, he had never seen the Flag handled with so much reverence and respect. I told DJ, with tears in my eyes, *"I don't know how or why but one day the Flag will be honoring you."* Then I hugged him as tears fell. I did not understand those words as I spoke them and I did not try to explain, I just dried my eyes."

We had lived with the threat of DJ going to war ever since he joined the Army. evil *(I will not capitalize the word because it does not deserve respect)* was rearing its ugly head everywhere. The only question was where DJ would be sent. He got word that in October, 2002, his company would be deployed to Guantanamo Bay, a naval base in Cuba, where suspected members of the Taliban are imprisoned. About this time DJ had informed me that he was having a pain that the Army medical personnel could not pin-point the origin; guessing hip, leg or back. The doctor's remedy was to give him pain pills. I knew that drugs just mask the real issue so I was determined to see him before he left for the two month deployment to give him some herbs to help rebuild any damage. I left immediately.

When I called DJ from Waco, Texas, which is forty-five miles north of Fort Hood, he could not believe it. *"You're where?!"* ..... *"No, you're not."* I told him I wasn't joking. I could hear friends in the background. Did I interrupt a party? Probably. The way I looked at it, they were leaving their home base and beginning a new chapter in their career as American Soldiers. He sounded panicked. He was not ready for his mom to come to his barracks. He and his buddies were packing things up that they would not be taking to Cuba and partying while they did it. I tried to relieve his concerns and told him not to worry about me, I did not come to intrude. I would connect with him later. So the next day we got together for lunch. He was looking forward to this new mission except for how hot it got in Cuba – 120 degrees! But it was good training for his next deployment, Iraq. I did not want to think about that yet, Cuba was all I could handle for now. I was happy just to see his face and to have time together. With lunch winding down, he was thinking of what we could do but I said,

"No, it's your last night in the States, go enjoy it with your friends."

He protested because he felt badly I had driven so far but finally agreed. We would see each other in the morning, on base in the Raider Gymnasium, the site of his departure.

In the morning, families started gathering outside the barracks, but then we were told to go to the Raider Gym, across the street. We were growing impatient to see our sons-husbands-fathers, when finally the long awaited moment arrived. Soldiers began arriving. Waiting... looking... and then there he was – seeing him walk in so tall and handsome warmed my heart. I was so proud. We sat down on the bleachers as he continued to make sure he had everything. As DJ's buddies walked by, he would introduce me but again I could not tell you one name. I was just focused on being able to touch him and look at him. A professional photographer took our picture as we sat on the bleachers. DJ later discovered that it was posted on the Fort Hood website, which meant a lot to him. And because it made DJ happy, it made me happy, too.

I wanted to put my arm around his waist but that was not an option because of the heat. So I settled for my hand on his knee. He never got used to the heat of Texas and I knew that the heat in Cuba would be a challenge. My hand was getting in his way as he had his rifle and other things. I apologized for the inconvenience saying,

"You will need to just put up with it because as long as
I can touch you, DJ, I will."

He just smiled his beautiful smile and replied,

"No problem."

I think he was happy to oblige his mom's request. I'm usually not a touchy-feely type of person but for some reason I had this inclination to touch him and never let go. I look back on this scene with gratitude and I give God all the glory.

A short ceremony, a pep talk really, and then we were told to say our goodbyes. The soldiers were to move to the other side of the partition that divided the gym in half for final instructions and we were asked to leave. I did not want to let go of his knee. I did not want this time to end. But on the other hand I could not have felt prouder to be the mother of this young man who had chosen this job, this vocation, as an American Soldier. Reluctantly, I did let go and received a hug, as tears welled in my eyes. As he walked away he turned to wave one last time. Then my tears came. I looked around for someone to hold, like you do in a *family* setting, for I truly feel I am part of a bigger family, thanks to DJ.

> *"Lord God, our strength and salvation, put in us the flame of Your love and make our love for You grow to a perfect love which reaches our neighbor"*(Ps. Prayer Vol II Divine Office pg 1161).

I spotted a young mother standing with her newborn in her arms; her face was all wet from tears. I walked over to console her and to find strength in our mutual sadness. Looking down at her I realized her cross was heavier than mine. Her baby was missing bonding with *"Daddy"* and the new mom was losing broad shoulders on which to rest her head. I prayed that her guardian angel would fortify her as she faced long nights alone. This image will be forever in my memory – two hearts trying to console each other when the only one that can is walking away. But we must never underestimate the power of love when the cross comes into our lives. Love can console, strengthen, and unify – love never ends.

> *"For when I am weak then I am strong"*(2 Cor 12:10).

I left an angel at Fort Hood to help fill the needs of the hearts of all families that are waiting for their loved ones to come home. And then broadening my view to every United States Military base there is in the world. May Angels help protect all who selflessly give their lives to defend the freedom of all American citizens.

Communication with DJ was sparse during this time. But I kept telling myself that, *"no news was good news."* I did receive this email:

Fri, 29 Nov 2002   12:23 – *I talked to you this morning* (I do not remember any details about the call) *but I forgot to tell you I need the addresses of everyone. Aunts and uncles and grandparents, please, and Phyllis, too, because I have a card for them all. I will try to write Andrea* (She was getting married and he was chosen to be best man.) *but it would be faster with a phone number. I tried to get in contact with her but I haven't succeeded, it doesn't mean I don't think about her and everyone else every day.*

I have chosen not to drink down here which has disappointed some except me. They think I'm more fun that way but I still manage to have fun when I am off. I don't want to have any regrets when I come home. I want to make the best out of the situation. **(And his buddies continued to call him, "SUNSHINE").**

*"Let your **light** shine before men in such a way that they may see your good works, and glorify your Father"*(Matt 5:16).

Speaking of coming home, add two weeks to Paul's birthday and that's the day (He was able to be home with us to celebrate Christmas and New Years before going back to Fort Hood). *I will see you again. I hope.*

Love, DJ

DJ said they had a colored flag system to warn them of the temperature. The coolest was green in the low 80's to black which meant it was over 120 degrees. I can't even imagine! There were reptiles from snakes to four foot long iguana lizards. The beautiful color of the water really captured his attention and sparked a new past-time – snorkeling. So when time permitted he took a disposable underwater camera to take pictures of his swimming companions, a huge array of tropical fish. I am only sharing the picture I liked – the picture he took of himself. He enjoyed snorkeling so much he was thinking of scuba diving someday. I was grateful that in-between his job he could relax and enjoy the beauty of God's creation.

Beauty is all around us, if we but open our eyes.

"Open his eyes so he may see"(2 Kgs 6:17).

18

Everything growing from the earth, bless the Lord.
You springs, bless the Lord.
You dolphins and all water creatures, bless the Lord.
All you birds of the air, bless the Lord.
All you beasts, wild, and tame, bless the Lord.
You sons of men, bless the Lord(Dan 3:57-88).

I was happy that DJ did make it home for Christmas on the 19th of December, 2002. We took our family picture immediately for the Christmas cards – a family picture without DJ would not be complete.

He did not share with me what he went through while in Cuba, only his pictures. The kids joked with him, *"These look like pictures Mom would take."* This was because there were pictures of sunrises and sunsets, which always caught my eye, too. I like the reminder to keep my eyes on the *"SON"*. I treasured these since they came from DJ.

In his explorations, he discovered a shrine to Blessed Mary. **(Our Lady of Charity,** *Patroness of Cuba, a Gift from God to Cuba: two men and a slave boy saw a white object, floating on the waves slowly coming toward them. It was a statue of the Virgin Mary holding The Child on Her left Arm, with a gold Cross in Her right Hand fastened to a board with the words, "I AM THE VIRGIN OF CHARITY." Sworn testimony of witnesses say that though it was in the water, The Virgin was not wet or Her clothing. Cubans consider Her their Image of Freedom.").*

This picture moved me more than I could express because I knew that our heavenly Mother was presenting Herself to DJ and he was accepting Her anew. I had been placing my son under Her protective Mantle ever since he left for boot camp and lighting candles by Her altar at church. I had my children involved with this sacred tradition too. She was my eyes and arms, and now confirmed by the pictures DJ took, She heard our prayers. I was filled with gratitude for a sign confirming God's love for our family.

One of my gifts for Christmas for all my sons were different elaborate Lego sets some containing hundreds of pieces. My only requirement was they had to be completed that day. So the race was on! I went around taking pictures as they worked on their sets.

I now look at these pictures and draw a deeper meaning. The pieces, laying on the floor or in the boxes, looked like chaos but when you follow the directions, they make something awesome. Like life, we have a certain amount of time on earth and at times it can get very chaotic. God knew this so He gave us Laws as directions to guide us so at the end of our lives we will see we were a *piece* of God's awesome Plan.

"'For My thoughts are not your thoughts, neither are your ways My ways', says the Lord. 'For as the heavens are higher than the earth, so are My ways higher than your ways and My thoughts than your thoughts'"(Is 55:8-9).

DJ asked me to take him to the airport after his Christmas break. When we arrived at the airport terminal entrance I parked the car by the curb. There was no way I could have him just jump out of the car and wave bye. I already felt badly that I could not go in and sit with him until his plane left. I got out of the car and received a hug that I will treasure forever. These moments are what makes being a mom worth every sacrifice. Tears came to my eyes and began to flow easily, which surprised me because I usually kept them between God and myself. But I had no control over them. They just came. I looked at him and said, *"I love you, DJ"*
He nodded and said, *"I love you, too, Mom."* And we hugged again.

This was my last moment alone with my son, Donald Laverne Michael Wheeler, Jr.

My eldest daughter and her boyfriend announced their engagement months before the holidays. We were hoping DJ would be at the wedding, since he was to be the best man. But the troops being deployed were in lock-down to prevent any soldier from developing cold-feet and try to opt-out from their deployment or AWOL (Absent With Out Leave). So here was DJ's first experience dealing with the only reason why he did not like the idea of joining the Army. Let me explain. Before leaving for boot camp, with tears welling-up in his eyes, he shared,

"Mom, you know the hardest thing about joining the Army is I'm going to miss all the birthdays, graduations, and all the other family times together. When I get back everyone will be all grown-up."
I responded with confidence,
"I know, DJ, but God will honor you in this sacrifice because He knows how hard it is for you. You can trust that."
Was the still, small, Voice speaking through me? I believe so because even as I spoke I felt at peace and trusted the words which reaffirmed for me that DJ would go and fight in Iraq and come home safely.

One of my Old Testament Heroes is Elijah. It had not rained for years but with *confidence and trust* he knelt and humbly prayed for rain and through perseverance God answered his prayer. (Story in 1 Kgs 18:41-46)

The thought of having a family event with him not there was too unbearable. I needed to be able to look around and see his face. So I had an idea. I found a company that could take a photograph and make it into a big five foot full body picture of DJ. I chose the one I took at Easter with him looking so happy in his Army uniform. I let him know of my plans and that he would be *watching* over all the festivities. He really liked that idea and could not wait to see it. He even requested that people, *"Dance with me!"* It made him laugh, which made my day. *Our lives intertwined so to bring joy and laughter.* The way I looked at it was if I could relieve just a little of his stress I was doing my job as a mom.

We placed "DJ" behind the bride and groom chairs at the head table – the center of attention, just like he would want it. When it came time for people to toast the new couple my boys began to chant, *"DJ, DJ, DJ, DJ, DJ!"* while pounding on the tables. All of a sudden I felt like I was lifted out of my chair and found myself running to position myself behind DJ's picture and began speaking, using a deeper voice, and it went something like this:

"Good evening, everyone. If you don't know who I am, let me introduce myself. I am one of Andrea's nine brothers, DJ. I must apologize for not mingling with everyone. I'm stiff as a board! All I can say is I should have listened to my mom's wise advice – stay away from booze! But, of course, I had to learn the hard way. Sorry, Mom." (laughter broke out) *To the happy couple, Andrea and Jake. Let me apologize for not being much fun tonight but we have had many good times in the past – in the mountains, swimming, and so many other good times you and I will always treasure. We*

will hold them forever in our hearts. I love you both so very much.

And the love of this great family that fills this room flows out the doors and through the city, over the hills, across the States and is felt here in Fort Hood. If this great love could be in all families, it would change the world and there would be no more wars for anyone to have to fight. It will sustain me during this time of separation as I begin this Mission with my fellow soldiers to face the evil in Iraq. I thank you again for your love and for your prayers. It will protect me until we meet again. God bless all of you and God bless America!"

There was laughter and tears – everyone thought I had staged it and that the speech was written on the back of the picture. Nothing could be further from the truth! I had never contemplated speaking for DJ. Those words still administer to my own heart whenever I think of them – that is why I believe it was the still, small, Voice that animated me and spoke through me. Later that evening, I was summoned to the phone. It was DJ and he was crying as he said,

"Thanks, Mom, for speaking for me. I couldn't have done as good a job as you did."

"Oh, baloney, DJ. You are a good speaker and when you get home we all will be listening, just waiting to hear what you will have to say"

"I'M KEEPING MY WORD, DJ." (Explanation in Introduction.)

DJ knew he would be going to Iraq. It was just a matter of when – *time*. He told us he had inspected his Bradley for the Mission. I call it "his" because he was the driver and he was responsible for it. It was to be loaded onto a train to be taken to a ship with its final destination Turkey and then DJ would drive it into Iraq... waiting and waiting. *Time ticking away.*

"...there is an appointed time for everything..."(Eccl 3:1-11).

He was told they would be leaving March 30, 2003. I was motivated, once again, to make the long drive, out of love for my son and for what he was about to do. Six of his siblings came along. When we arrived, we contacted DJ, who told us the orders had changed. Now they did not know for sure when they would be leaving. *"Soon,"* was all he was told. The motto I have heard DJ use since joining the Army is, *"Hurry up and wait,"* and another more Godly saying is, *"Patience is a virtue."* My personal favorite is, *"It's all good."* Praise God, we had *time* with DJ and that truly was good.

I was ready for a long overdue family vacation. Whenever DJ could get off from his duties, I gave him the "wheel" - the best tour guide ever! He took us to places that he had been with his friends. All the while I would take picture after picture, even when DJ was just leaning against a pole. That is when he said,

> *"Mom! I'm just standing. Why are you taking my picture?"*
> *"Because I can. You're here. I can see you. I want pictures."*

*Thank you, Holy Spirit, for prompting me to do something that I now treasure with all my heart.

Whenever he had to report back to base he always made the rounds making sure everyone got a hug. A whole week of hugs! What a blessing we had this *time.* Our lives intertwined and strengthen each other with the glue that holds families together – LOVE.

DJ was finally informed they would be leaving at 4am on Thursday, April 3rd. All week I had not gone to daily Mass, but Wednesday I awoke to the still, small Voice. So I quietly slipped out from my room without waking the kids and headed for the closest Catholic Church, Saint Joseph. About ten people were gathered before Mass to pray the rosary. For years I joined in saying the morning rosary at my parish so I felt at "home." Today when we reached the 4th Mystery, an elderly Mexican gentleman made eye contact, motioning that I should lead it. With all the people to choose from, he picked me. What an honor! We were saying the Sorrowful Mysteries on a Wednesday because it was Lent so the 4th is "Jesus carries the Cross." Was this merely a coincidence? Well, since I don't believe in coincidences, no. God was working here.

Let me explain. Back on August 23, 2002, I was saying The Stations of the Cross. I started the 5th Station, "Simon helps Jesus carry the Cross", I *"felt"* the Cross on my back and I looked to my right and *"saw"* Jesus, His Face – dirty, bruised and bloodied with the Crown of Thorns encircling His Head. A scene so real I saw the Blood flowing into His eyes, which were filled with such sadness. Jesus pierced my heart with His gaze, beckoning me never to leave. The cross is something no one wants but sometimes, like Simon, we are forced and life is forever changed.

I have since read a book, Our Lady at Fatima: Prophecies of Tragedy or Hope? by Antonio A. Borellie Machado, who did a study on the apparitions of Fatima and wrote,

> *"Our Lady calls not just one Simon of Cyrene, but many, multitudes, even legions of them. Fatima was not just an appeal for three shepherd children to do penance. This appeal was directed at the whole world"* (pg. 93).

I pray when the weight of the cross is placed on our shoulders we all, like Simon, become saints.

The gentleman asking me to lead the 4th Sorrowful Mystery, The Carrying of the Cross; meditating on Christ and His last walk before He is crucified. In retrospect, I believe God, my heavenly Father who cares so much for me, was letting me know the Cross would be coming into my life in a big way and He was preparing me. God was tiling the soil of my heart so to be ready to receive His Grace to accomplish His Work. The gentleman had no idea what part he was playing in my life but nevertheless, he was a *piece* of God's awesome Plan. *Evidence of the still, small Voice animating men who are willing to do His Will.*

After the rosary, Mass began. When it came time for the homily, the priest spoke these words,

> *"Seek the Lord and make a commitment to Him. Don't be lukewarm. And remember sacrificing during Lent combats not only evil in our lives but also evil in the world - so evil will not be able to affect us."*

He reminded me that this Lenten season DJ and his buddies would literally be going into the desert with Jesus, their Savior, and doing physical combat and it would be longer than forty days. I shared these words, as was my routine, with the kids and they listened respectively.

4am, April 3, 2003. The plan was to get there early to have time to take pictures – *time, precious time.* We arrived around three-thirty and there was a lot of activity. Soldiers running up and down the barracks stairs. They were checking and rechecking their uniforms and gear while family members tried to stay near them. You could feel the excitement and from my perspective, nervousness and anxiety.

We found DJ and began following him around like puppy dogs. I was not concerned about what the others wanted to do, I just needed to be as close to him for as long as possible. The soldiers began forming into their respective companies, talking and laughing. We stood back at this time and only watched. Then the command was given, *"Attention!"* like only the Army can say it. All was still and the soldiers were straight backed and eyes forward.

DJ is in the front, 2nd on right.

Then my mother's heart came to the surface. Not only did I look at my son, but I looked at all the soldiers and I was overwhelmed. What amazing men and women! I have been around and watched young people for many years. Coming from a large family and being involved in many school activities especially sports. All these experiences help teach an important quality called teamwork. This teamwork really shows up when you see soldiers, everyone moving in unison. In some sports you will find quite a number of the team standing on the sidelines waiting for their turn to be in the action. The military is different. Everyone is part of the action. Every soldier would be involved in this, the biggest event of their lives. No one was going to be left standing on the sidelines just watching. No one would be sitting this one out. They joined and with courage and fortitude they would be seeing this Mission through to the end. This experience would test their 'mettle', the very core of who they are, and change them for the rest of their lives – if they are blest to have the rest of their lives. Yesterday, their biggest concern was where to eat, whose house they would watch the big game, or what new computer game to buy. Today they are off to a war in country they may have heard about in geography class or in the news. I wanted to take all of them and hug them and never let go.

The enemy these soldiers were going over to Iraq to find was none other than the dictator, Saddam Hussein, a modern day Hitler.

Since 1945, countries joined together under the title of the United Nations which created a set of rules and laws that all agreed to obey. Hussein thought he was above the law, for over a decade, and planned to continue thumbing his nose at the world. Now my son and other young men and women, who were proud to be American citizens, were ready to put their own lives on the line to make this "Hitler" stop his evil. What heroes, all of them! The Army was not just a branch of our military defense system, it was my family. These soldiers were *my* children. Not one hair on their head had better be harmed!

A sergeant's bellow woke me from my thoughts.

"You will be going over to the Raider Gymnasium where there will be better lighting so your families can get pictures and hugs."

Darkness was looming around us, which made this *time* even more somber. Bright lights would be greatly appreciated. We were excused as he had more things to say to the soldiers. I moved slowly. I kept turning around so I could keep my eyes on my son. It was like I had to fill a lifetime of looking at him in these moments. *Do you think the still, small Voice was animating me again? As I look at it from this vantage point, I know He did.* Then they began their march to the

gym. I wanted to get a picture of this but it was too dark, so I settled for the lobby of the gym and waited. I watched all those faces go past me. I wanted to embed them in my heart. Then I saw DJ and took a picture I will treasure forever. A determined young man set to go on a Mission. Willing to lay his life down, if need be, and do whatever he was ordered so as to defend his country and his fellow comrades, his buddies – his family now.

We congregated on the bleachers. He began pointing out some of his buddies – Jarvis Gibson and William Velez; a couple of names and faces I will never forget. Velez would be with DJ as he drove the Bradley Fighting Machine into Iraq. *(DJ would correct us if we ever called the Bradley a "tank" because it was so much more).* We met a commanding officer and his family. In a stern and threatening voice his wife addressed DJ, *"You better make sure you know what you're doing! I will hold you personally responsible if anything happens to my husband!"*

I could not believe my ears! Such selfishness and fear coming from a seasoned military wife. Should I tell her husband, *"You better not give my son a command that will get him killed!"* No, of course not, because being in the military means they are part of a team – like none other. DJ and I never had an opportunity to speak about this conversation, there was no time.

Between the introductions and laughter, I tried to remain thankful that I had this time, but it was hard, so very hard. I did not want it to end. Time was running out... *Time...* sure enough, the announcement was made to say our final goodbyes. *Time was up.*

There were more pictures – pictures of hugs from one sibling after another. I took every one as they gave their support and love to DJ. Then a soldier asked if he could take a picture of all of us. That was very much welcomed and would be treasured. I thanked him for his kindness. *Did that still, small Voice motivate that man? I think so.* My

heavenly Father knew that I needed that family picture with DJ.

Now it was my turn to give DJ a hug. Everyone was waiting - looking at me. I couldn't do it. I paced and with tears welling-up in my eyes I said,

"How do I let my little boy go off to face so much evil?" DJ stood there watching me – waiting for me. I continued as tears fell, *"This is not what a mother is supposed to do!"*

DJ, upon hearing that, laughed and with great love and compassion engulfed me in his arms and said,

"Don't worry, Mom. I'll be back."

I clung to him. I never wanted to let go.

"I know. I know you will, DJ."

I lingered longer in his embrace and I found peace. *I go back to that moment even now for comfort.* As our embrace ended, but still close to each other, I asked, as I wiped my tears away,

"Are you sure you have everything?"

Patting his left chest pocket DJ said,

"I have my rosary and my prayer book. It's all I need."

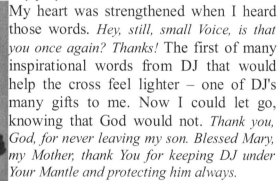

My heart was strengthened when I heard those words. *Hey, still, small Voice, is that you once again? Thanks!* The first of many inspirational words from DJ that would help the cross feel lighter – one of DJ's many gifts to me. Now I could let go, knowing that God would not. *Thank you, God, for never leaving my son. Blessed Mary, my Mother, thank You for keeping DJ under Your Mantle and protecting him always.*

Faith – how do those who do not have faith in God live? Times like this really make you realize that you should never take anything for granted. How you should protect your faith, like the

"treasure hidden in the field"* or *"pearl of great value"(Matt. 13:44-45) from anyone who wants you to doubt His existence or anyone who would ridicule you for it. They are the enemies that we face in our daily lives, just as surely as Saddam Hussein. Doubting in God and His love for us is what His opposition wants us to do. In moments like this you can feel the spiritual energy all around – real and tangible. I praise God at this very moment for allowing me to have experienced such a time. The cross was really near, but closer still was God, His Saints and Angels.

At this time we were told to leave and wait outside. I don't remember talking to anyone as we exited the building. What words could be spoken? This morning was too hard to experience, let alone trying to find words that would help. There were no words that would take away the pain of this reality. You just had to experience it, flow with it and hand it over to God's Mighty Hands.

Walking outside I cannot recall if it was actually still dark or not, all I remember is I welcomed looking at the light of the street lamps. *Keep my eyes on the Light of God.* My spiritual instincts were kicking-in.

"Lord, kindle a light for my guidance and scatter my darkness"(Ps 18:28).

There were several buses lined-up waiting to take our precious cargo away from us. The sound of the motors was disturbing to me. I wanted them to go away. Give me more time with DJ, *Time.* The soldiers had to stay inside for final instructions before boarding the buses which would take them on to a jet, or would it be a train? I didn't have answers to those questions. The Army did and I prayed they would always consider what was best for my son. Then after several minutes, the soldiers started to march out. With every soldier that passed, the still, small Voice let me know what I was witnessing. I could feel the presence of Guardian Angels hovering over them and so I began to recite a prayer I have prayed since I was a child:

Angel of God, my guardian dear through whom God's Love
permits me here. Ever this day be at my side to light,
to guard to rule and guide. Amen.

I was confident the Angels would. Later I remembered a song that perfectly explains what I witnessed:

Oh, when the Saints go marching in,
Oh, when the Saints go marching in,
Lord, how I want to be in that number,
When the Saints go marching in.

I have since seen many soldiers line-up and board buses to face their Mission and that song continues to give me comfort. I am firmly convinced soldiers are modern-day saints, ready to die for you and me, the American Citizens. Pray for them daily.

It was hard to distinguish which soldier was DJ because of all their gear. But then we spotted him some of the kids walked a few steps with him but others stood back, one here, another there, and watched. That is what I chose to do, too. I began to have flashbacks of all the mornings I would stand outside and wait with the kids to board the bus, waving as the big yellow bus pulled away from the driveway

30

and watched the little hands rise-up and wave back. Then when school got out, I would be back out there to greet them as they got off the bus and listen to all their experiences of the day.

DJ would not be coming back in just a few hours to tell what he had learned. My little boy did not need his mother's hand any longer. He was a man. A man of whom I am so proud – an American Soldier. Someone that I admired and respected. I had no idea when I would even hear from him. My desire was to grab his hand, hold on tight, and make him stay or take me along. My hands stayed at my side but my heart went with him. The sacrifice of love.

DJ sat on the side facing us so we continued to look at him. Every so often, as he would talk and laugh with his buddies, he would glance at us. It was so very hard. The little boy who could barely see out the bus window was now so grown that his chest was totally visible above the window. He still had a backpack, but his little baseball cap was replaced with a helmet, which he had taken off upon entering the bus. How... how could this be happening? When will it be the time for me to greet him back home...to touch him...to see him smile? Questions no one could answer today. *Under the Cross look for Jesus.*

One final wave, the red from the taillights, the smell of the exhaust and the distant hum of the motors. Then stillness broken only by some sobbing and whispering. My time to hold my son was gone. Now was the time to be far from embraces but never far from my heart. Life should have stopped right then and there. I wanted to say to my extended Army family, *"Let us all agree to stand right where we are until they come back. We will begin a prayer vigil for their safety and never allow anything to distract us."*

I wanted that to be our communal agreement. How could any of us proceed as usual when their Mission was war?

It was Thursday, April 3, 2003.

CHAPTER THREE: IRAQ MONTHS

The waiting game. When will they be able to get to a phone or when will the mail have an envelope with his handwriting? I was so anxious. I wanted to see all that he was going through to better understand how best to pray for him. My faith in God sustained me. I called on the Angels and Saints to protect my son and his buddies. I knew they were on duty because I felt the still, small Voice reassuring me. *Praise God!*

It was weeks before we heard from PFC Donald Laverne Wheeler, Jr., my son, the soldier. The waiting was very hard. Knowing he was in a very unsettled and volatile country made it even harder. Let's recap some of the stark realities of this war:

- The country of Turkey had opened their borders then changed their mind. Kuwait, the country south of Iraq, agreed to receive the ship carrying our Troops equipment. That is my guess what caused the delay from a March 30th deployment to April 3rd.
- DJ's Bradley was on a ship waiting for him, and since he was the driver of this Fighting Vehicle, he had the responsibility to drive it over the border into a country that manufactured terrorists and was an extension of the Syrian Desert.
- The soldiers had been trained in chemical warfare, along with weapon handling and the constant threat of roadside bombs, IED's (Improved Explosive Device) and enemy gunfire.
- Temperatures were well over 100 degrees. When you add in the heat generated from the Bradley's motor in a vehicle and remember there is no luxury like air conditioning, it must have made this trip feel like purgatory on earth!
- Sand was everywhere, seeping through the cracks of the vehicle and getting into their eyes, nose, mouth and everywhere else.

Back on the home-front, after planning a wedding now there was a high school graduation, so I was preparing food and freezing it. I did it all with love in my heart for my children and in particular the one graduating and the one at war. I united our actions for the intent to glorify God. Then one joyful afternoon, around two o'clock, the phone rang and the faint voice of DJ was on the other end! I ran to the dining room, thinking because of all the windows the connection would be better, and now I was looking at our brick cross, (10'x6'x3'), in our front yard, which I had constructed just before my third sister died in 1991. Looking back, God used this moment. He inspired me, through His still, small Voice as the phone call proceeded, to throw myself, a great sinner, at the foot of the Cross. I realized all I had experienced in my life, death of two sisters in my teens, a miscarriage, another sister's death in my thirties, to list a few. Now because of DJ I am brought to this moment and by the Grace of God I experienced a peace that was filled with Love and Joy more than I had ever known. My son, at war in Iraq, was on the other end of the phone! The conversation went something like this:

"Hi, Mom, how are you?"

"DJ? Is that you?

"Yes, it is, Mom."

"Oh, DJ! How are you?"

"I"m fine but I can't talk long..."

Then some static and fading out and in. *"DJ, I can barely hear you."* Then the connection went dead. I spoke to the dead air, *"It was good to hear your voice, DJ,"* tears welling up in my eyes, *"I love you and pray for you every day,"* I continued saying in a whisper. I looked at the phone to hit the off button, and then looked up to thank God that I finally heard my son's voice. He was okay! Then the phone rang again. It had to be DJ.

"DJ?"

"Yeah, it's me. We have a lousy connection and I only have a few minutes."

"Oh, I am just grateful to hear your voice again. Are you okay?"

"I'm okay. We're doing fine." Then his voice went real low, *"There was an accident and my buddy died right in front of me."* Then just as fast his voice went back up to his normal pitch, *"But don't worry. We're doing okay. How are you, Mom?"*

"Doing much better now that I hear your voice. You have no idea."

"Tell me what you've been doing,"

"I've been cooking for your brother's graduation party and just try to keep going. But I don't want to talk about me. Tell me where you are?"

"Well, we can't. Not until we get the "okay". I will be writing to you soon, so you will have an address. Oh, could you send me a rosary book. I misplaced mine."

"Of course I will. It will be the first thing I pack.

Pray the
ROSARY

33

Let me know what other things you need and I will get them to you as fast as I can."

"I'm getting the signal that I have to go and let someone else use the phone. Wet ones. We need wet ones. Tell everyone that I love and miss them."

"We love you, too, and miss you. Take care..."

He cuts me off, *"Really have to go. I love you, Mom."*

Phone goes dead. *"I love you, too, DJ"* I pushed the off button and then stood, staring out the window at the Cross, hanging onto the phone, as I lowered it in front of me. There was so much to try to understand. He needed a rosary book because Pope John Paul II just added the Mystery of Light, the Luminous, and we all were still learning it. How appropriate since DJ was shining the Light of Christ through his *star* in Iraq. But I still had no idea where he was on the map and if he was still traveling. Earlier I had web-surfed and found a phone number putting me in contact with a woman at Fort Hood who said, *"Somewhere north of Baghdad."* But could I trust this stranger? Oh, well. I chose to concentrate on the fact I heard DJ's voice. Now what about his voice? His reference about, *"my buddy died right in front of me."* He talked about it briefly and in a whisper – I assume so others would not hear but he took the chance because he needed me to know. I now

DJ's buddy,
1LT Osbaldo "Baldo" Orozco

knew a way to help. I would surround DJ with extra Angels that would help him remain focused and soften any of the memories associated with the death of his buddy so it would not turn into nightmares and interfere with the Mission. I knew my Savior would not let me down and that Blessed Mary's Mantle would continue to envelope him. I had great confidence and peace because I knew God would answer my prayer. I focused on the beautiful fact, DJ called! I had heard his voice. *Thank You, God!*

Life continued but it was like I was holding my breath in between phone calls. I would take a big exhale after the phone calls, in praise and thanksgiving to God that I heard his voice, and then with the next breath, began "the waiting game" all over again. I treasured the letters he sent. I could feel the warmth of his love. To touch something DJ had touched just a few weeks earlier was like getting a hug. I could see him folding the letter, licking the envelope, sealing it and then holding it or putting it in his breast pocket as he went to mail

34

it. It was something familiar for me to visualize. Trying to imagine him carrying a gun and mounting a Bradley Fighting Machine was way too foreign.

This is the first letter from Iraq. DJ forgot to put a date on it so I can only guess that it was written before April 26, 2003 Baldo's birth into Eternal Life.

Hi, how you doing? Things are going well here. We've been in Iraq for a couple weeks now. It was weird to go through the cities and towns and see all the children and adults line the sides of the streets with smiles. We've been in some little battles but everyone's fine. Now we are just doing patrols and trying to keep the peace. Wondering if you could send some candy and HiC powder for me and the guys. The food here is getting kind of bland. Pray for me and tell everyone I said Hi. Please send me my address book. I love you and will pray for you.

Love, DJ

PS. Sorry for the handwriting, in a hurry.

9 May 03

Hello. I'm doing fine. We moved into one of Saddam's houses (the headquarters for 4th Infantry Division) *about three days ago. It has running water and shade. My section stays on the balcony. It's on the second floor. It looks like a stadium with all the seats. I haven't got your letters yet, the mail is messed up. I received Wes' package* (close friend and cousin) *2 days ago. Mail's the best thing we get over here so please keep sending it. I'll try to write as much as I can. I love all of you. If you could send me a couple dollar bills to give to*

some of the children running around here   *I love you. DJ*

P.S. The thread was perfect. (per phone for sewing patches on his uniform)
Send baby wipes. (written on the envelope)

35

Saddam Hussein's palace in Tikrit, which became the Headquarters of the 4th Infantry Division. The 4th ID sign to the right of the center.

Steps and doors DJ more than likely used in Tikrit, Iraq, 2003.

Later CPL Velez told me DJ was offered the best bed the Army had to offer, a cot, when he was the driver. He declined. He ended up making his own bed from the cushions that were bolted on the stadium seats in the castle and lined them up on the floor.

Pictures from
http://122infantry.org/pics/iraqifreedompagefour.htm

As my seventh child's high school graduation was fast approaching, I couldn't imagine another party without DJ. So the big picture of DJ was set up again right by the door so everyone would be greeted by him. I also put a basket with blank cards and envelopes with the address he finally gave me. I put a note on the picture:

CONGRATULATIONS, QUENTIN!

You know you are all in my thoughts and I ask you to pray for me. I don't get enough mail and have almost no telephone time with family so if you would, please, tell me about this day and anything else you might want to share. My mom will mail it for you.

God love you all! See you when I see you.

Love, DJ

Here I was speaking for DJ again, just as I did at the wedding. Boy, I couldn't wait for when he would be home and I could just sit back and listen. It was a way for me to remind people not to just go about their daily life without remembering DJ and his buddies. Here we were partying while the reality was that men and women in uniform were facing events that constantly put their lives in danger. In a conversation with DJ he said,

"We've been working very long hours with barely time to sleep."

This is a different kind of war. Our military is at a loss to even recognize the enemy. In other wars the enemy's uniform alerted you. But the tactic of this enemy is to look like the people the military are trying to help liberate. It could be anyone who walks up to you with a smile on their face and the next thing you know they detonate a bomb they have strapped to themselves. But we can help. During WWII our nation had a list of goods that were rationed. Everyone complied. This war I call on all of us to rationing – rationing time to get on our knees and pray. Prayer is the most powerful weapon we have. A saying I have heard is,

"God governs the world, but prayer governs God"

(PIETA prayerbook pg 18).

DJ was a man of God who was praying – an unbeatable combination.

DJ called a few days later to talk to his brother that had graduated with the hope that the party went well. He *even* apologized for not being able to be there, like it was *his fault* he couldn't make it. I handed the phone over to him so they could have their privacy.

One Saturday in June, upon arriving home from Mass and buying groceries, my youngest told me DJ had called. I just sat down and cried. My heart hurt. There was nothing more important to me than being able to hear my son's voice and I had missed the chance! There were no words. My youngest just stood there looking at me. I apologized to him as I sobbed and asked him to bear with me because I really wanted to hear what they talked about. Taking a few deep breaths I was able to collect myself so he continued,

"We didn't talk long. DJ just said he was doing well and hoped all of us were okay and that he loved us. And that's about it," and starting to walk away he turned back and said, *"Oh, yeah, he wants more baby wipes."*

I thanked him for telling me and he went on his way. I sat for a few more minutes. And then later, alone in my bedroom, the floodgates opened up – the reality of my world. On my knees, I asked God to take all my actions of every day as an offering to help protect my son. I knew He would.

Shortest letter I ever received from DJ and very touching:

26 June 03

Hey Mom, I'm writing to say I'm alright and miss you. I called last night and missed talking to you again. I'll try in a couple of days. Hope you are doing alright. I am. It's just pretty hot over here. Sorry for the handwriting. In a rush. All of a sudden got to go.

Love you.   DJ

At this point I developed a new routine which involved trying to stay at home as much as possible because I couldn't stand hearing I missed DJ's calls. We had an answering machine and I would play them over and over just to hear his voice but he needed to hear our voice, too. So I would stock up on supplies for DJ's packages and my weekly groceries. That way I was home as much as possible and still able to make sure at least one package got shipped weekly and letters mailed two to three times a week, all different times. It was my way to help him feel connected to home so to keep his spirits up.

DJ's unwillingness to share with me many details about his daily life continued and I began to understand why. When you are forging ahead, trying to stay strong, you don't want to keep recalling your reality. So diverting the conversation to what I was doing made it easier for him. He could picture the things I would talk about because it was all happening in our home or at the schools he attended. So in his mind's eye he could conjure up a different surrounding and mentally take a "vacation" from his reality. I can only guess at this because he never complained to me about anything.

38

Though I remember one phone call on a Saturday afternoon in July when he was in a rare agitated frame of mind. He took issue with one of my letters when I said I was happy that he was having some down time and asked him where he went to see live music. I was only going off what they showed on the website for Fort Hood, Charlie Company. He needed to set the story straight,

"I don't know who is attending those live music concerts or having down time to play games but it certainly isn't us. We are working 24 hours a day, 7 days a week since we got here. We try to sleep but it's more like cat-naps and then we are up again."

I was shocked and then ashamed of myself for believing what I found while searching the web. Since DJ didn't share his personal experiences with me I was desperate to know. So it helped me to think he was playing billiard or cards and listening to music now and then. But now I was left with the unfamiliar again. Instead of his red pickup truck, a Walkman, and baseball cap, he was mounting a Bradley with a rifle and helmet – the unknown, the unimaginable. My eyes desperately needed pictures of what he was seeing. My niece suggested that I send him a disposable camera. So I did and included an envelope in which he could send it back. Much later we did finally receive them back. Looking at the pictures was overwhelming because I could feel DJ in me looking at them too. His eyes were picking what scenes would make a good picture and I can only imagine the words he called out to get his buddies to look at him. It became very real to me.

"Hey, guys."
"Yeah, DJ?"

As they turned to look at him, he took the picture... *They turned and looked at him.* They could *see* DJ. Their eyes were looking at him and now my eyes were looking at them. I *so* wanted to be in their shoes. I want that experience again.

"Hey, Mom!"

and when I turn he will be standing right in front of me. I will see his smile and hear his laughter. Moments caught in time that were really

39

insignificant then but so very important now. Daily moments we take for granted. Moments stopped in time – time here and time gone.

In the following letter DJ affirmed where he was drawing all his strength.

27 July 03

Hello, hope you all are doing well. Thank you for all the goodies. Very good to have something normal to eat and something good to drink. I think I'm set on baby wipes for a while. But the koolaid runs out fast. Powder detergent to wash my clothes. It has to be powder cuz I use the sink to wash them. I was promoted to Specialist on June 1st so on the letters it's SPC Wheeler not PFC. For some reason I keep forgetting to tell you when I talk to you on the phone. Tell Trevor, Thomas, and Quentin to get in touch with me. I know they know how to write. Andrea, by the time you get this you'll probably already had your baby. I bet it's a boy and it's already 8 pounds. (The baby was a girl, born on August 9.)

Pray for you all everyday by saying the rosary.
It's the only way to stay sane out here.

With all that's happened so far and still to happen. My family – my inspiration from dad and mom all the way down to Patrick. Everyone unique in their own way. When it gets hard to deal with this place I pray for all of you. Each one in their own battles in life – to some of yours makes this seem easy. But be strong. It'll all work out in the end.
Love, your son and brother
DJ
PS. Can't believe I wrote all that!

As I read this letter tears came. I knew my son had encountered God on a deeply personal level and the Holy Spirit helped him write the letter. I knew when Specialist Donald L. Wheeler, Jr. got home he would continue to lead us and encourage us to seek and to love God on a more personal level, too. We are in a battle just as surely as DJ, though we are not reaching for a rifle and an Army helmet. The battle is the choices we make. We need to ask ourselves are the choices serving God or His enemy?

"Your adversary the devil prowls around like a roaring lion,
seeking someone to devour" (1 Pet 5:8).

*"For the gate is narrow and the way is hard that leads to life
and those who find it are few"*(Matt 7:14).

It is the only way to true salvation and freedom. DJ's last words, before he left for Iraq, should be true for all of us. Patting his breast pocket that held his prayer book and rosary he said,

"It's all I need."

The annual county fair, August, 2003, opened and my daughter and her husband asked me to go. I declined the invitation because I had to stay home to record the news for DJ. The evening news had a story, amazingly, about the 4th Infantry in Tikrit, Iraq *(the city where DJ finally told us he was stationed)*. It showed the soldiers traveling by way of a Bradley which gave me a feeling of being in one. (*This was the visual I so desperately needed!*) It showed them going from building to building trying to turn up any hidden ammunition and/or hiding places of Saddam Hussein. While the report was running, I was struck how the back of one of the soldiers looked like DJ. Then the camera was set-up at the bottom of the stairs while the soldiers rushed up the stairs. As the profiles of the soldiers went quickly past another soldier made me think of DJ. I knew I would have to review this broadcast. Out of all the broadcasts of the 4th Infantry's activities, this was the only one I ever had the desire to watch over. *Was this the still, small Voice? Well, you decide.* The first soldier, whose back made me think of DJ, after reviewing it, I quickly concluded it was not DJ. Moving on to when the soldiers were rushing up the stairs, I had to use the "slow" button to get a better look. The profile of a soldier showed the tip of his tongue extended between his lips, a family trait of some, when intent on what we are doing. It had to be DJ!

I looked for verification from my children. The first one said, *"No, it isn't him."* Some said they did not know DJ's profile well enough to say one way or the other. But finally two concurred with my suspicion. Looking back on this day I need to make something very clear. I was never in the habit of sitting night after night taping the news. But it was my custom to always jump at an opportunity to be with my children. So I do not take any credit for this incident. I praise God for caring about me so much as to lead me to be available to see that report. I now have my own home movie of DJ doing his job in Iraq, all because my Father in Heaven is in the details of my life! Later DJ confirmed the incident but did not add any more details.

IMPORTANT NOTE: On **July 11, 2012** I found a web site for 1-22 Infantry dated August 7, 2003. I am positive this soldier, though not identified, is my handsome son doing his job! Now I have a snapshot of the incident, too!

**A forever Vigilant soldier,
SPC Donald L. Wheeler, Jr.
and the continuing evidence of
GOD'S MIGHTY HAND in my life!**

9 Sept 03

*Hello. How's everyone? I hope good. Here in Tikrit it's nice and hot. The nights started to get a little cooler, which is good. It's been 5 months now and still no word on when we're going home. We've had a lot of guys get out of the Army over here so we're low on bodies to help out. So everyone's picking up the slack. They picked me and a couple of other guys to do a ceremony for General Sanchez. You probably saw him on TV. He's the Commander of all the troops in Iraq. He shook my hand at the end of it. Then about three days later Rumsfeld came, Secretary of Defense, and gave a speech at Division which is down the street from us. While everyone else got either to attend it or relax they had us Infantry outside the compound blocking all the streets surrounding the compound to avoid attacks while he was there. But the day after I got back from the General's ceremony they moved me to the **gunner's** seat of the Bradley so now I shoot instead of drive. It's kinda like being promoted. We've been pretty busy of late and the phone I used to use is broken. So that's why I haven't called, sorry. My Captain wanted us doing patrols in the Bradley every hour so we didn't get a break from that for 4 days. Now I'm on dismount patrols which is we walk through the city looking for trouble makers and IED's, which are Improvised Explosion Devices. These bombs that can be remote detonated. We have problems with these of late. They messed up a lot of people and vehicles. No one's been killed by those yet so that's good.*

Thank God. SOMEONE is watching over us over here. I can feel HIM.

Andrea, I'd be honored to be Caylee's Godfather. I'm so happy for you. (While DJ was gone he became an uncle. He had been so happy and excited about the baby and was looking forward to holding his goddaughter and requested a picture which was already in the mail.) *I wish I could have been home for the past couple months. It's been life altering for a lot of you. Mom, thank you for everything you've been doing for me over here. It makes my day to hear from you. It means a lot more than words can express. I started to take pictures again. It's been a while but I've got like four of them to waste. I think that's it for now. Talk to you later.*

Love, DJ

PS. If you could, I find it easy to write everyone else with little cards like the one you sent last time. (Little cards with their own envelopes)

When I read the words, **"I can feel Him",** I knew God had heard my prayers, reaffirming my trust in Him. He was with my son. My son could *feel* Him. I cried many tears – tears of gratitude and love. DJ's deep awareness of God walking with him through the most challenging months of his life because he was being obedient to his duty as a Soldier, persevering under great hardships, and had the discipline of unceasingly praying from his heart. It was very clear to me I need not be afraid for him because God, our most loving Father, Brother and Consoler, was with him.

> ***"...the peace of God, which passes all understanding, will keep your hearts and your minds in Christ Jesus"***(Phil 4:7).

18 Sept 03

Hello Mom and everybody. How are things going? Things are going smoothly over here. Thanks for the kool aid. The chips and dip were awesome. The cookies made it all the way here intact. (My attempts to send his favorite peanut butter cookies resulting in crumbs, causing DJ's buddies to comment, "DJ, are you so hungry that you are resorting to eating sand!") *I'm not really eating candy any more but the children here love the stuff. They moved me to the gunner's seat on the Bradley so when we go through Tikrit in the daytime it is always like a parade. The kids crowd the streets. It is crazy how many kids these people have but the men have 4 wives so I guess that is why. But to have all these kids running around and still be so violent. They try to avoid attacking us when we have a crowd around us so as not to hurt their own, but it still happens. They told us to look forward to April for going home. But they said something about taking leave out of here for a week or two. So we'll see. Also for now board games are how we spend our off time. With "Risk" – it's kinda played out. That's why I asked for "Axis and Allies" also if they have a football game that looks good and if Burt has an idea for a game like Axis and Allies or something else. Oh, about the leave they said the people that go the only place to get a flight is to Baltimore and after that you find your own way home but we'll see when it gets closer to that day.*

Well, time to go. Love you all. Miss you.

Love, DJ

My granddaughter/goddaughter was baptized on October 4th and everyone came to witness the newest member of the family become a child of God. So the next day, October 5th, when DJ called, almost everyone had the opportunity to speak with their brother, fighting a war halfway around the world. What a blessing! I remember standing in the living room and seeing three out of the four that were talking to him. I was missing the opportunity, for the moment, to hear DJ's voice, but it was a sacrifice I gladly made so my children and his dad could speak with him. I had, in the past, talked to him more times, so it was only fair. One of my daughters shared that she asked him,

"What do you do all day?"

"I get shot at and it never ends."

She was speechless for that real frankness. He had never talked that way with me. Was it his need to protect me? Why? I could handle the truth. We always knew the seriousness of DJ's vocation and now with his confession of the daily danger we could, with more clarity, lift him up in prayer. When I finally got my turn I said,

"Wasn't it nice to be able to talk to everyone?"

"Yes, but it's funny, Mom, your voice is the only one I can hear clearly."

I told him that one day he'll hear all of us clearly. He informed us that he might be getting a chance to come home maybe by the end of the month. That just made my day – wow! Then he shared that he had been promoted to **gunner** of the Bradley but kept forgetting to tell us. *(The last two letters dated September 9 and 18 we did not receive until after October 13th).* Another job I could not visualize but it did not stop me from being very proud of him. Later we were informed by Lieutenant Colonel Russell, who knew and fought alongside DJ:

"It was unheard of for anyone to be given the promotion at nineteen months. It really showed DJ's dedication."

DJ certainly was proving he had found his vocation and nothing would stop him.

Time was up and he had to go.

SUNDAY, OCTOBER 5, 2003
THE LAST PHONE CALL FROM DJ.

44

CHAPTER FOUR: OCTOBER 13, 2003

SATURDAY, OCTOBER 11

We wcrc in Steubenville, Ohio for a son's high school football game - they won!

SUNDAY, OCTOBER 12

The next morning we went to the Chapel for Mass on the campus of Franciscan University, also in Steubenville, where my daughter was a student. I arrived by myself forty-five minutes early which is my custom. During this time the still, small Voice brought to mind two of my sons, one being DJ. I had developed a habit, if you haven't noticed, to pay attention to that Voice. With the two names of my sons being raised to God in prayer and placing extra Angels around them I continued my Sunday worship. While praying and praising God, I was flooded in love. A love so real and personal that tears flowed as God, my Father, Brother, and Consoler, my All, engulfed me. God's Love produced such peace and joy that tears would come and go throughout the Mass. What a glorious and timeless experience whenever I recall that day. I am very humbled. *Looking back it reminded me of the times with DJ at Fort Hood and the Flag raising experience and the airport scene.*

MONDAY, OCTOBER 13

After my three o'clock wake-up call by the Lord to say the Divine Mercy Chaplet, and falling back to sleep, my alarm woke me at my usual five o'clock. I began my daily chores: laundry, picking-up the TV area, saying my prayers, and then made the school lunches.

By 6:15 my morning routine was done and I heard music alarms going off and saw lights. The two youngest came down and began eating their breakfast. I grabbed a bowl of cereal and headed for the VCR and the morning news, just a few feet away. I kept up with taping parts of the news for DJ's homecoming. The remote lay in my lap and my cereal bowl was in my left hand. As a spoonful of cereal was making its way to my mouth I hear,

*"A **gunner** in Tikrit, Iraq has been killed. Details to follow."*

The spoon stopped in mid-air and that still, small Voice told me,

"It's DJ."

My hand was steady and calm, but my mouth could not receive the food. I slowly lowered the spoon back into the bowl and then did a thing not allowed in my house, I put the bowl on the floor. It felt like the blood had stopped flowing in my body and the weight of the bowl and spoon were too heavy. I felt numb. I could not pick up the remote to begin taping and I could not tell you any more of the broadcast other than they did not disclose the **gunner's** name, *"pending the notification of next of kin"*.

My interior conversation began, *"Stop being so paranoid...I've been watching too many news programs and now I'm over reacting...I'm just overly sensitive....The word* **'gunner'** *is new to my mind because DJ just told us last weekend that he made that promotion, so now the word is jumping out at me...Stop being filled with such doom and gloom!"*

After I was through reprimanding myself, I thought it was time to say our family prayers and lay all of this at the altar of the Lord. In the mornings we either say the rosary in front of our family altar or, if we are running late, we would say it in the car, which was the case this morning. I had sat much too long. I have thanked the Lord many times for our morning ride to town because it gave us time to say the rosary. Today was another one of those times.

I had made the decision not to tell the kids about **the gunner**, no need to worry them. So when the eldest of the school kids was leaving for career school I asked him to remember DJ and his buddies in his prayers. Then it was time for the rest of us to leave. In the car I said,

"Hey, I have an idea. Let's say this rosary for soldiers and in particular for DJ and his buddies."

The kids agreed. DJ's vocation gave me, as a parent, many opportunities to speak about the virtue of compassion. We should never be so far removed that we cannot feel the pain of others. So we gave DJ and his buddies to the Lord.

We were now ready for the day. The doom and gloom had left and I felt joy-filled as the first two got out at the high school. Then at the elementary school, one more got out, and the last one at the middle school, a couple miles across town. I then attended the nine o'clock Mass at the church back by the elementary school.

Once at church, I had forty-five minutes to prepare to receive Jesus. My routine involved buying and lighting a candle by Blessed Mary's Altar to remind Her to give DJ a hug for me and place him under Her Mantle. I knew She would – She's a Mother after all. Then I walked The Stations of the Cross and then going into a pew I read the Mass readings then quiet adoration and/ or start the rosary. After

46

receiving Jesus and Mass concludes, His Peace flows over me and I am renewed.

My errand for the day was to go to the bulk store. The news story; "the **gunner** in Tikrit" surfaced once more at the checkout counter. The clerk, being new, asked how many children I had because of the amount of food I was buying, which lead me to talk about DJ and his Mission. I asked her,

"Please keep all the service men in your prayers because we can only imagine what they go through daily. We know what is normal for us but we don't have a clue as to what is 'normal' for them."

She was very sympathetic and said she would. I loaded up my car and headed for home.

When I got the groceries put away I was able to enjoy a visit from my eldest daughter and granddaughter. I told her about the news report and from that conversation I decided to go on-line and see if there were any details. After trying for a while all I could find was an article. I printed it so she could read it and then left it on the counter in the kitchen for the other kids to read about "a **gunner** in Tikrit" when they got home. We then sat down to rest and pray.

When it was time to get the kids from school, my daughter walked with me to the kitchen and was leaning on the counter as I walked behind her, heading to the sink. All of a sudden I stopped and turned to my left to face the window to the backyard and began a sentence I did not know I wanted to speak. The scene went like this: While pointing my right index finger at the window, I said,

"There's a black hole ahead of me and I don't want to go in it but I'm going to have to."

I looked at my daughter who just stared at me. I did not try to justify or explain those words. There were a few moments of silence and then putting my hand down I resumed my walk to the back door and whispered,

"I have to get the kids."

With that I was out the door. As I walked to the car I said out loud,

"What was that!!"

I wanted to spit – to somehow wash my mouth out for having spoken such ridiculous words. They didn't belong to me. They were foreign to my mouth and to my thinking. *"Black hole?"* What's wrong with me, first for thinking that the **gunner** in Tikrit was DJ and now this. I handed it over to God because nothing made sense.

I picked up my son at the elementary school, who would need to come back to town later for his football practice and then my daughter and her two friends at the high school. My eldest son would bring home the other two after their football practice. On the way home I shared the **"gunner"** story. I thought it would not hurt the two friends to walk a few minutes in the shoes of a family that has a son and brother in the Army, who is walking where most of us would not want to go and was putting his life on the line every day. I said that we needed to pray for all of them then turned on the radio so they could talk about whatever teenage girls like to talk about, while I caught up with my son and listened for any more news.

Arriving home my daughter took her friends to her room and then came out to get snacks which I was setting up. While she waited I said,

"You know the 'gunner' probably isn't DJ but we know a soldier did die and we need to pray for that family. We know a family somewhere today will have an Army man coming down their driveway to give them the heartbreaking news. And from all of this we can learn to be more compassionate. "

She nodded her head and said thanks as she picked up the snacks. I reminded her that I would be leaving with the youngest for his football practice in a few minutes and to behave themselves. She said they would and headed to her room.

By six-twenty most of my family was home except for the youngest. A few of us were in the kitchen when the phone rang. My son, eldest of the students, answered it. It was my daughter at college. Knowing the news came on at six-thirty, I excused myself because I needed to hear if there was any more information on the **"gunner"**. As I was saying this I walked into the living room to "my" rocking chair *(the one I rocked most of my babies)*. I sat down and picked up the remote to be ready to record when I noticed it had gotten very quiet in the kitchen but I figured my daughter must have a lot to share. My thoughts were interrupted when my eldest daughter said,

"Mom, you have to go to the door. Someone's here."
"Someone else can go. I have to hear the news."
"No, Mom. You have to go."

The thought came to my mind that my husband must have sent me flowers and the delivery man needs to put them in my arms. *(Now these were truly my thoughts – forever hopeful).* With a smile coming to my lips I stood and turned and saw my daughter to my left. Looking at her sad expression and her face drained of color, my smile left my face and I whispered,

"It's DJ?"

She nodded her head as tears filled her eyes. I reached out and touched her arm and then I headed for the front door. The still, small Voice had warned me all day for this news, so my walk was slow and steady.

The interior door was already opened so I was able to see a man in a uniform coming up the last two steps of our front porch. He stopped and turned to look behind him because there was a woman also in a uniform – *that uniform,* the green uniform the Army called Class A's. The last time I saw one DJ was wearing it at Easter, over a year and a half ago. *DJ smiling and joking.* I opened the screen door and walked out. He looked up. I asked,

*"Is it all right if I touch your uniform? The last time I saw it
my son was wearing it."*

He nodded. I touched the buttons on the front pockets. I spoke as I read, *"Johnson?"*

"Yes, Ma'am. My name is SGT Johnson and this is..."

I know he introduced the woman soldier, too, but I was lost in the moment. We shook hands. I asked as I stepped back, *"This is about DJ?"* My eyes were longing for my son to be standing before me.

"Yes." He continued, *"I regret to inform you that your son was killed...."* or whatever it is they say.

God had been telling me all day, **"It's DJ"**, preparing me for this moment, and here it was. **"The gunner in Tikrit".** I remember nodding and being still. I noticed there was someone in the foyer so I asked them to get their dad. I just stood, looking down at the cement and waited. *DJ, my little boy.*

Then the door opened and DJ's dad stepped out. He received the same formal speech as I continued to look down. After he composed himself I asked if they would tell our children. Out of respect for our children I felt it was necessary for them to see the uniform that DJ had worn and to hear the formal speech we had just heard, like so many military families before us. I hoped it would help them to be able to face the reality that their brother would never come home. I also felt it was the Army's responsibility to see all of DJ's brothers and sisters and understand what he gave up when he chose to become an American Soldier. *May we never take our freedom for granted.* The officers nodded. As I led them into the living room I said, *"We have several children and it might take a while to get them all here."*

"We will wait for however long it will take," he said as they sat down on the couch, *"Don't worry about us."* She nodded in agreement.

"Thank you for understanding."

I turned and headed for the kitchen. I hugged my daughter and thanked her and my son because they already had in motion the task of getting their siblings home. The youngest had to be picked up so his dad had already left. I headed back into the living room and asked if I could get them anything while they waited. They again said not to worry about them and to take care of myself and my family. I apologized for keeping them from their families. They told me that they were married and were prepared to stay for hours if that is what I needed.

I didn't know what else I could do so I began a slow pace in the living room where the officers were because this was where I usually did my praying. So I began to pray, asking God to help me make sense out of what was happening. I was not crying because I was still trying to grasp how this could be true. *Never to see DJ again?!?* Then I thought of my kids... how will they react? *How could there never be another moment with DJ again?* I had been through this when two of my sisters died in a car accident when I was fifteen and again, when I was thirty-five, another sister died due to a tumor on her liver. I know first-hand what it is like to lose a sibling. The pain – the hard reality of Death. My thoughts were interrupted by someone saying they got ahold of everyone, except one, but would keep trying. Again I turned to our guests to apologize. My daughter's friends were leaving, because I remember looking out the living room window and seeing a car I didn't recognize arrive and then leave almost immediately. Then I was told that a son was leaving. I hurried into the kitchen and yelled out the window to stop him. He said he was going to find the one that wasn't answering his phone. I asked him again to stay so the officers would not have to wait longer. He reluctantly agreed.

As we were speaking, his dad's arrived home with my youngest and as he came into the kitchen we hugged. We walked together to the living room. Now it was time for the formal family announcement. Within forty-five minutes we had everyone except a son and a daughter. It sure was a blessing that the daughter had been on the phone when the Army officers arrived. God was showing His Fatherly care because someone would have had to call her instead she was *with* us. Her friends arranged to bring her home, a five hour trip. One friend would drive her car and another one would follow, that way they could turn right around and head back without missing their classes.

I still couldn't believe this was really happening! Walking in the the living room I informed the officers that we have most of our children here as they followed me and sat down. Yes, the kids knew already but it was important that the Army show SPC Donald L. Wheeler, Jr.'s siblings the same respect they showed his parents. So the officer stood up in the middle of the room and gave the same speech that I was now hearing for the third time. I was sitting at the end of the big couch, looked at him and then at the floor. *DJ couldn't be dead! I was holding on to the hope that they were wrong.* I still did not cry. The kids listened in between a few sobs and blowing of noses but mainly quiet – quiet pain, quiet tears, quiet acceptance.

After the Army officer was done with his formal speech, he paused and then said there were some papers that we had to sign. Pointing as I got up, I suggested we go to the kitchen where the lighting was better and a counter to place his papers. I led the way. I stood at the end of our counter and the officer placed his papers down. I just watched. I really do not remember if anything was being said at this point but I did notice the last son had arrived and his pain was visible. He made me wonder *what could I do to help?* This Cross of grief became a personal journey. For me, at that point in time, I was following the directions of the officer. I think everyone had followed us into the kitchen for this, the business side of Death, and yet it still was quiet. I recall DJ's dad standing to my right and the officer was on my left. He said something like he needed our signatures to verify that we knew that our son was dead, or something similar. He told us the Army had assigned us another officer with the title Army Liaison Officer(LNO) that would contact us with further details. Then he pointed on the paper where I needed to sign and I obeyed.

Then the still, small Voice told me to ask him his name. I knew the Voice was not talking about his last name because I had read it above his right pocket. I thought the idea was silly, *"I'll be lucky if I remember his last name, let alone his first."* But I was obedient to the Voice.

51

"Would you please tell me your first name?"

He had been standing quietly watching us sign the paper, and now he looked at me with a frown that told me it was an unusual request. Urged on by the Voice I continued,

"I know it probably goes against Army protocol, but would you humor me, please?"

Another pause and then he said, ***"Michael."***

As the name *"Michael"* was spoken, the still, small Voice asked,

"Will you Trust Me now?"

There was a resounding ***"Yes!"*** inside of me, which instantly showed on my face as I smiled. All those Divine Mercy Chaplets that I had been praying for years and years came flooding over me. My total and complete Trust in God was rooted deep within me. It is the core of who I am – the air I breathe. My ***"Yes!"*** came without hesitation. Of course I would Trust the Lord! I knew the Lord had not forgotten to protect my little boy and Blessed Mary, with Her Mantle wrapped around DJ, did not abandon Her post of shielding him from harm. Even though it looked like Death had won, this was all a part of a bigger Plan. God was at work here and He was asking me to let Him. I smiled and began laughing and crying, all at the same time, shedding my first tears – tears of Joy! I reached out to hug him saying,

"Thank you! You have no idea how much your name means to me."

And then I addressed the kids, *"I don't know what the Lord is doing, but what I do know is if we continue to Trust Him, He will show us. DJ is in His Hands and Good will come from this."*

The Officer looked shocked. There was no way to explain to him what God was saying to me. "Michael" was standing in front of me, confirming that DJ was with God. I felt the Cross lift at that very moment. I could face whatever God had in store for me – *black hole* and all. I could rest assured that this was all part of God's Plan. As DJ had written,

"Be strong. It'll all work out in the end."

Even those words from his letter sound very similar to the words Saint Paul wrote to the Philippians 1:6, ***"I am confident...the One who began a good work...will bring it to completion."***

I have encouraged my family to read that Letter in the New Testament, to give them the strength they need as they go on with their lives. God's Love Letters, written to all of us so many years ago, and DJ's words in his letters were inspired by God too. I can say this because of the courage and peace I find when I read them. I believe DJ was listening to the still, small Voice because even at the end of his letter he wrote,

"I can't believe I wrote that."

I CONTINUE TO PROFESS, *HE* DID NOT.

On October 13, a date that was not only my son's birth into Eternal Life but it is also the Anniversary of the final apparition at Fatima. *Fatima.* The beginning of DJ's life pointed me to Fatima and now his last day on earth points me to Fatima. The apparitions began with the Angel of Peace, Saint Michael appearing from April to October, ironically the same months that DJ was in Iraq. The final apparition where tens of thousands of people could not believe what they were witnessing as the sun began falling toward the earth. Just like I felt when I was told the news of DJ's death. But as the sun returned to its place in the sky, their faith in God was renewed – my heart reversed from sadness to joy when I was reminded by the still, small Voice to continue to Trust Him. I, for my part, would persevere in prayer, our greatest weapon against evil as Blessed Mary, our Mother, reminded us,

"Pray, pray, pray."

October 13, 2003, the earthly journey of my son, Specialist Donald L. Wheeler, Jr., came to an end. His life intertwined with mine for twenty-two years and I am better for having been blest with the experience. DJ found praying,

"...the only way to stay sane."

He *listened* for God and could,

"...feel Him"

as he wrote in his letters. His buddies who journeyed with him those last months of his life felt the effect of his deepening faith and were changed by the experience. Some came to know God, others renewed their faith in God while others began to discover a deeper relationship with God. The greatest gift DJ gave was the example of finding the time to listen to that still, small Voice. I challenge you to learn from my son and his buddies, the American Soldiers. Discover prayer and be open to change. The still, small Voice is beckoning and my question to you is,

"Are you listening?"

The rest of the evening of October 13th we spent making phone calls to DJ's grandparents, aunts, uncles and cousins. After allowing enough time for whoever could join us, I led everyone in praying one of the most perfect of all prayers after the Holy Sacrifice of the Mass and the Divine Office, the rosary. DJ kept strong by praying it and so would we.

I mentioned the Divine Mercy Chaplet, prayed at the 3 o'clock hour. Here is an explanation from Jesus to Saint Faustina (1931-1935):

 *"Tell the world about My Mercy and My Love... The flames of Mercy are burning in Me. I desire to pour them out upon human souls. Oh, what pain they cause Me when they do not want to accept them...Tell aching mankind to snuggle close to My Heart, and I will fill it with Peace...Tell (all people)...that I am Love and Mercy itself. When a soul approaches Me with Trust, I fill it with such an abundance of Graces that it cannot contain them within itself, but radiates them to other souls"*(Diary by Saint Faustina #1074)

HOW TO PRAY THE CHAPLET OF DIVINE MERCY
(You can use a rosary)

1.) Make the Sign of the Cross.
2.) Pray: *You expired, Jesus, but the source of Life gushed forth for souls and the ocean of Mercy opened up for the whole world.*
> *O Fount of Life, infallible Divine Mercy envelope the whole world and empty Yourself out upon us.*
> 3 times - *O Blood and Water which gushed forth from the Heart of Jesus as a Fountain of Mercy for us, I Trust In You.*
3.) Pray the Our Father, Hail Mary and The Apostles Creed.
4.) On the *Our Father* beads/bigger beads/or beads by themselves pray:
> *Eternal Father, I offer You the Body and Blood, Soul and Divinity of Your dearly Beloved Son, Our Lord, Jesus Christ, in atonement for our sins and those of the whole world.*
5.) On the *Hail Mary* beads or smaller beads or 10 beads all together pray:
> *For the sake of His sorrowful Passion have Mercy on us and the whole world.*

54

6.) Repeat steps 4 and 5 for all five decades.

7.) Then repeat this prayer 3 times:

Holy God, Holy Mighty One, Holy Immortal One, have Mercy on us and the whole world.

8.) Final prayer:

Eternal God, whose Mercy is endless and the treasury of compassion is inexhaustible. Look kindly upon us and increase Your Mercy in us that in difficult moments we might not despair not become despondent but with greatest confidence surrender ourselves to Your most Holy Will which is Love and Mercy itself.

9.) Make the Sign of the Cross.

CHAPTER FIVE *"...THOUGH I WALK THROUGH THE VALLEY..."(Ps 23:4)*

IMPORTANT NOTE: The following days included many acts of kindness from friends and strangers and many phone calls and news reporters.

TUESDAY, OCTOBER 14

One of the questions we had and thought would never be answered was when DJ whispered, *"My buddy died right in front of me."* We were praying for him about that incident and now resigned ourselves to never knowing all that DJ wanted to say.

3am, October 14th the phone rang. I answered, as I was already awake saying the Divine Mercy Chaplet. A man said, *"Are you the family of SPC Donald Wheeler, Jr. that died in Iraq?"*

"Yes."

"I served with him"

I immediately thought it was a prank call since DJ's buddies were still in Iraq so I said, *"Of course you did. Well, may God bless you and good night."*

I prayed as I hung up the phone, *"Please God protect us from such cruel people."* The phone rang again. I picked it up and the same man's voice was speaking quickly, *"Please don't hang up! I did serve with DJ in Iraq. I was with him. I didn't re-enlist, that's why I'm back in the States."*

He gained my confidence by telling me facts about their deployment. Then, without any provocation from me, he proceeded to tell me about the accident when their buddy died. I took notes. Through tears I told him how grateful I was for answering one of our questions about DJ's deployment. We thought we would never find out any of the details. As we said goodbye I recognized it as a display of God's great Mercy, as it was 3 o'clock, and I *can* Trust Him. God is good!

I stayed up to type my notes so I could print it out for everyone to read and thank God for this buddy of DJ's. It has since been misplaced and my memory of the soldier's name is gone, too, but he is held forever close in my heart. My recollection of what he shared about that horrific accident is that due to a dust storm, the first Bradley did not see a drop-off, flipped over, and the second Bradley, because of the driver's fast reaction was able to save them from a similar fate. The driver was SPC Donald L. Wheeler, Jr. (*Part of this was verified by letters SSG Robert W. Morris, page 62 and SFC Kelly W. Lucas, page 85*).

We received a phone call around two in the afternoon that same day, October 14th, from the same man, *"I don't know what got into me! I know there is a time change from California to Michigan but for whatever reason I made the call anyway. I'm so sorry."*

"Oh, don't apologize. It was God working through you to remind me to continue to Trust Him because you did call at the 3 o'clock hour, the Divine Mercy Hour. So thank you and don't apologize. God worked through you to strengthen me. Again thank you so much."

He had listened to the still, small Voice and he did something he normally would never think of doing. The "what" that got into him was God and all I can say is, *"Thank you for LISTENING."*

"My ways are not your ways, says the Lord"(Is 55:8).

TRUTH AND HOPE. The funny thing about hope, I never wanted to let it go.

"Now faith is the assurance of things hoped for, the conviction of things not seen"(Heb 11:1).

I found I was still hoping that they had gotten this all wrong. So when our Army liaison officer showed up the first thing I wanted was to have the truth verified. He said that soldiers that give the ultimate sacrifice go to Dover, Delaware so I wanted him to speak to someone in Dover that had proven medically that SPC Donald L. Wheeler, Jr. was in their building. He said he would try. Then I thought why burden him, I could go to Dover myself. He could give me the address of this place and I would go through every door until I found DJ, *if* he was there and that was a big *if* for me. Besides I had promised DJ when he got back home I would be there to greet him. Though Delaware was not home it was the United States and I wanted to honor that promise. I had to pray about this and within this quiet time I felt DJ saying,

"Mom, I'm okay. You need to stay with my brothers and sisters. They need you now."

So that was my answer. I needed to stay home but I still wanted that phone call made to someone who actually touched my son in Dover. *Hope against hope.*

WEDNESDAY, OCTOBER 15

I asked the Army liaison officer, *"Have you gotten any information from Dover?"*

He replied, *"No, but I have something for you."*

He had in his possession a set of dog-tags. I saw DJ's name on them. *Oh, my gosh. Then DJ was really gone.* As I held them they were something I associated with DJ wearing. I passed them on to the kids as I wondered if this was enough verification. DJ *is* really gone. Reluctantly I began to surrender my last shred of hope. *Oh, the struggle within my heart!* But then I heard the kids exclaimed,

"These don't say Roman Catholic. DJ's did."

What? As I came out of my inner-struggle, I looked at the officer and asked for an explanation. He confessed they could not find DJ's dog-tags and so they had these made. I was having a hard time believing this officer's ability and now he admitted to lying to us. I wanted him replaced with someone who cared about the truth. Don't waste my time with lies, not when we are talking about the *possible* death of my son. But I was overruled and was told to just let him do his job. I thought his "job" was to help the family of the soldier who gave the ultimate sacrifice. Lying to them was not an option – not in my mind. But then I began to look at the positive side of the situation. If they did not have DJ's dog-tags and they could not get me medical verification, that meant there was a good chance that DJ was not in Dover. *Hope was back!*

> *"While he was still speaking, there came from the ruler's house some who said, 'Your daughter is dead. Why trouble the Teacher any further?' But overhearing what they said, Jesus said to the ruler of the synagogue, "Do not fear, only believe"* (Mk 5:35-36).

THURSDAY, OCTOBER 16

I no longer cared if the liaison officer was at the house or not. The phone call to Dover for medical verification was still not done and knowing he was capable of lying undermined his credibility. Plus I was dealing with interior struggles: *Could God really let this happen?* The example DJ had set for all of us – selflessly serving our country during a time of war spoke loudly to all of us. What were we willing to do to help fight the evil that hit our world? Go on with life as normal or step-up and *do* something? On top of this I began to hear people in my own house saying since DJ was named after a great-uncle that died in Korea it was fate that DJ would end up the same way. *Unbelievable!* I let people talk because my focus was not diverted. Truth was my goal and hope remained.

"May the God of hope fill you with all joy and peace in believing, so that by the power of the Holy Spirit you may abound in hope" (Rom 15:13).

God continued to show His love and compassion by not one but two priests with military background, our pastor and a pastor three miles away. They offered to make sure everything was done to adhere to military protocol for DJ's Catholic funeral. I was so grateful, words failed me. That allowed me to concentrate on the eulogy. This idea came after I received a phone call from a mom in California on October 16th. She said she was determined to talk to me and after a variety of phone calls finally succeeded. She needed to tell me about her son, Adam. He called her from Tikrit, Iraq, crying,
"My buddy, Wheeler, died today! I don't know how I am going to survive this place without him!"
My words to her came without hesitation,
"You tell Adam that DJ has not left him or the Mission. He will be with Adam, watching from a better vantage point, to protect and guide him and all his buddies until they all come home."
I spoke with great confidence, assurance, and a clear vision. I surprised myself. God made me realize that more people might be feeling defeated and grief stricken. It was up to me to inform them not to give-up or give-in to the grief but to stand strong and *Trust in God* because the battle was not over. I *had* to speak at the Mass and try to convey this confidence for all to hear. This incident also answered another one of our questions, *"Who was the last one that DJ saw before going out on his Mission that early afternoon?"* DJ had gone back into the headquarters to get his helmet and it was Adam who saw him for the last time and got DJ's last wave and last smile before mounting the Bradley. God is good!

FRIDAY, OCTOBER 17
The Army liaison officer arrived with news.
"The body of SPC Donald L. Wheeler, Jr. will be flown into Detroit Metropolitan Airport late tonight."
What!? How could this be? He had told us he had not been able to talk to anyone who could medically verify they even had DJ but now he has the time of his arrival into Michigan. *What was going on!* I

was motioned into the dining room for a private meeting. *Now what?* Once inside, a family member confessed that the officer had told him on Thursday that they had verified that it was DJ and he made the decision to keep the Truth hidden, leaving the rest of us in the dark for over 24 hours. *Blackness develops when Truth is hidden. The beginning signs of the "black hole."*

I wanted the truth and now I had an avalanche of Truth. First: DJ had indeed been in Dover, Delaware, so I needed to let go of the hope that I had been clinging to all these days. Second: DJ was scheduled to arrive in Michigan in just a few hours. How do you prepare to "welcome" your son who has given the ultimate sacrifice? The only way I have learned to approach any cross in my life – hand in hand with the Lord and pray, pray, pray.

"Even though I walk through the valley of the shadow of death I will fear no evil, for You are with me; Your rod and Your staff comfort me"
(Ps 23:4)

In order to share this experience I will again use part of my words that at spoke at the **"Fallen Heroes Memorial Concert"** that was organized and performed by Kelly Trudell and Company to honor DJ, Matthew Soper, Brent Beeler, and James Collins, Jr. on March 6, 2010. (http://www.kellytrudell.net/)

On October 17, four days after DJ's birth into Eternal Life, we were at the Northwest hanger at Detroit Metro Airport waiting to receive DJ as he returned to Michigan. Out through the huge hanger doors came his coffin on a gurney. All I could see though was the American Flag. We processed behind as he was wheeled toward the waiting hearse. That is when the words that I spoke to DJ flooded me:

"SOMEDAY THE FLAG WILL BE HONORING YOU."

I had to walk faster to catch up with DJ so I could touch his Flag, my way of thanking it. The Flag had been covering my son, SPC Donald L Wheeler, Jr., from Iraq to Germany to Delaware and now home to Michigan. This Flag was alerting all Americans who bothered to notice, that here lies a soldier who gave his all for you, your family, and your friends. **Honor him**.

The Flag: The Stars, represent the souls of those who serve. The red and white stripes represent their blood, sweat and tears. Their ALL.

So when you see the American Flag, please remember our sons; DJ Wheeler, Brent Beeler, Matthew Soper, and James Collins, Jr. and all the military who gave their tomorrows for your todays.

(My youngest, wearing his ROTC uniform and would be my 6th son

60

to enlist in the Army, was standing beside me holding DJ's Flag case and together we opened it). This is our Flag given to us to honor DJ. So God did fulfill those words *"Someday the Flag will be honoring you"* because He is forever faithful and true and I can TRUST HIM. And I choose to TRUST in the words DJ wrote, too,

"Be strong, it'll all work out in the end."
And I vow to do just that.

We were the first car behind the hearse and I was deeply engrossed in keeping my eyes on its back window. I wanted to catch every possible glimpse of the Flag that was honoring DJ during the hour ride to the funeral home. The words I spoke to DJ sixteen months ago, by the inspiration of the Holy Spirit, were being fulfilled before my eyes. Not the way I had envisioned – DJ holding an important position in the Army that would place him in parades to be honored. But, *"My Ways are not your Ways,"* says the Lord. I had lost hope just a few hours earlier but now the Lord seemed to be telling me to not let that hope go and continue to trust Him. So I made a decision to stay in the moment which meant, for now, to keep my eyes on The Flag. While I was praising and thanking the Lord I also prayed that I would not get in the way of His Mighty Hand and the Plan He had for my family and me.

SATURDAY, OCTOBER 18
It was very early by the time we arrived at the funeral home. I walked behind DJ as he was wheeled into a side parlor. I cannot tell you what was going on around me, I only saw the coffin. They had taken the Flag off for safe-keeping. Placing my hand on top, I began a very slow walk around it, feeling the cold metal against the palm of my hand. Just under my hand laid my son once so full of life and adventurous. DJ trained himself to be an American Soldier to defeat the evil that had hit our world. Now my hand was resting on top of where my son's body was in repose. Here was the verification I needed. The Truth that SPC Donald L. Wheeler, Jr. had died. How could *this* be part of God's Plan? I did not understand.

With my walk around the coffin over, I did the only thing I knew, I took out my rosary and making the Sign of the Cross dropped on my knees and prayed out loud,

"I believe in God, The Father the Almighty, the Creator of Heaven and earth..."

SUNDAY, OCTOBER 19

The next day we had an unexpected visitor from California. The wife of 1LT Osbaldo Orozco, who died back in April, 2003, came to honor DJ! We couldn't believe it! Such a beautiful woman with a warm and generous heart. She is the epitome of what it means to be a military family. She also brought with her presents, pictures that Baldo had taken of DJ in Iraq. Pictures that gave me the visual that I had been praying for all throughout DJ's deployment. He looked so skinny which I expected since they would have been constantly on the move and sweating so much. But it was his eyes that touched me and gave me peace. They looked so blue. It was like he had indeed *"seen"* God and the encounter reflected in his eyes. Yes, the kindness of a stranger who is part of my "family" forever and will be forever in my prayers.

TIKRIT, IRAQ
SSG Robert W. Morris

Dear Sir and Ma'am,   October 17, 2003

I am writing you in regards to your son, Specialist Donald L. Wheeler. Please, allow me to offer my deepest condolences for the tragic loss of your son, as I too, will miss him deeply.

I met you on the eve of our deployment preparation, before we entered the gymnasium, on April 3, 2003. I was Donald's Bradley commander up until one month prior to being deployed to Iraq. He was not just my driver, but as a member of a three-man crew on our Bradley, he was my friend. Our crew was broken up when I was reassigned as a Squad Leader in the same Platoon, but we were able to maintain our friendship.

Let me start by saying that he was a Soldier by every means of the word. He had a clear image of his goals and set out to achieve them, which his recent promotion to Specialist confirms. I remember after the terrible Bradley accident in April, that claimed the life of our Lieutenant; DJ was a little skeptical of driving again, as anyone would be, but he knew and supported the mission, and did it anyway, because he did NOT let anyone down, ever. We talked about what happened that night a few times and he was always optimistic about it. I chose his Bradley to assign my squad and myself to, because he was the best at his job and I knew he would keep us safe. Your son provided a strong source of motivation for everyone around him and had many friends in the Company. His peers and his leadership, alike, looked to him for trust and camaraderie.

As leaders, we continuously search for the exceptional soldiers in our unit that stand out from the rest, take their own initiative, set the example, and have a natural ability to encourage others. Donald was that

62

man and was exactly who we were looking for. Specialist Wheeler was who we wanted to lead the soldiers of tomorrow and we hoped he would take the next step and join our Corps of Non-Commissioned Officers.

Donald is, and will always be, a member of a special caliber of men – Infantrymen. Infantrymen do not just volunteer to serve their country, they volunteer to serve, knowing that when they are called upon, they will go to the places that no one else wants to go and they will do the job no one else wants to do. When Donald was called upon, he answered loud and thunderously with pride, honor, and personal courage. Fear and challenges do not intimidate brave men like your son. Donald was dedicated to the men he served with and will be remembered not only as a soldier, an Infantryman, and a friend, but he will also be remembered as a Hero.

Mourning in front of 4th Infantry Headquarters in Tikrit, Iraq for DJ and SPC James Powell.

TIKRIT, IRAQ
Captain Bradley L Boyd
Infantry, Commanding

Dear Mr. and Mrs. Wheeler,   30 October 2003

May I express my sorrow and concern for you because of the loss of your son. I was Donald's Company Commander, and I know that nothing I can say will reduce the pain you are experiencing, but I wanted to write you and give you all the information I have about the day we lost Donald in Tikrit. That day devastated all of us in Charlie Company, and Donald's presence is missed by each of us every day.

The day in question was the 13th of October, 2003. The Salah ah din province had been beset by riots and demonstrations for the previous ten days. The province had also been saturated by Improvised Explosive Devices (IED) em-placed by enemy insurgents (Fedayeen). 1st Battalion, 22nd Infantry Regiment was being hit twice per day by these IED's and had lost one soldier in Tikrit, on the 1st of October. Her name was Private First Class Esparza. The city of Tikrit is the population and cultural center of the Salah ah din province, and Charlie Company is responsible for the security and defense of Tikrit. By the 13th, Charlie Company had already been hit by one IED with no casualties, and we interdicted two others before they were detonated. The company had also dispersed two riots in the city up to this point.

On the 12th of October I was issued an order from the Battalion Commander, Lieutenant Colonel Steven Russell. The order stated that there was the stray possibility of a violent demonstration in Tikrit from 6:30am to 3pm on the **13th**. We had already seen one of these large, violent demonstrations manifest themselves in the city of Bayji to our north several days prior. In Bayji, the enemy burned the governor's building and the police station. They also fired Rocket Propelled Grenades (RPG's) and machine guns at U.S. forces. The Battalion Commander's intent was for Charlie Company to prevent a similar occurrence in Tikrit. The key to preventing that situation was to have an aggressive presence at likely areas where demonstrators might assemble. By preventing the crowd from assembling, you prevent them from organizing, thereby preventing the riot. We also knew that anytime there are large groups of people, terrorists try to take the opportunity to make an example.

We anticipated that example to be in the form of an IED most likely or a direct fire ambush, which would be slightly less likely. In order to accomplish the mission of preventing the riot or demonstration while also protecting ourselves from IED's and ambushes, I took the 1st Platoon to conduct mounted and dismounted patrols in the target area. The target area was the outdoor Market in the center of town flanked by a large Mosque to the west. 1st Platoon began their patrols at 6:30am.

Your son was a member of the 1st Platoon. His call sign was Red Two Golf (R2G). This meant that he was the **gunner** for the Bradley Fighting Vehicle that was commanded by Red Two (R2). Red Two is Staff Sergeant Bordes. Your son's responsibility included the employment of the Bradley's armament: a 25mm machine gun that fires armor piercing and high explosive ammunition, a coaxial machine gun that fires 7.62 mm ammunition, and TOW missile launcher that fires a missile designed to destroy tanks.

On the **13th**, Donald was at his station in the **gunner's** hatch while Staff Sergeant Bordes was in the hatch on Donald's right. The Bradley they were in was providing rear security for the mounted patrol that his section was conducting. A section is two Bradleys. The lead vehicle is responsible for security to the front and the trail vehicle is responsible for turning its turret around so that it can see towards the rear. The two vehicles then move down the road, keeping a sharp eye out for anything suspicious.

The day was hot, about 100 degrees by 11am. The city had been very quiet. No IED's had been detonated or detected nor had any gatherings of rioters taken place. 1st Platoon's aggressive patrolling had in fact deterred any riot or demonstration that had been planned. By about 1pm the platoon was confident that they had accomplished their mission. Donald's section was continuing to patrol through the streets near the market-place while the platoon's other section was in another part of town near the Mosque. The platoon also had two squads of infantry on separate patrols in the same vicinity of Donald's section. I was in my own section of Bradleys about one mile south of Donald's section, conducting a patrol near the governor's building.

At approximately 1:30pm, a white pick-up truck with three Iraqi males in it stopped in an intersection behind Donald's vehicle. Two of the Iraqis had RPG's. They both fired at Donald's Bradley. **One RPG missed. We don't know where it went.** The other struck the turret of Donald's Bradley and he was killed instantly. Staff Sergeant Bordes was thrown down into the bottom of the turret by the force of the blast. The pick-up truck with the Iraqis in it sped away around a corner before the lead Bradley was able to bring its weapons to bear.

The platoon leader in the lead Bradley called me on the radio and told me that Red Two Golf was hit. I sped to the ambush sight as fast as I could. With me were my First Sergeant and the Company's Senior Medic. I was on the scene within a couple of minutes. I positioned the Bradleys in a tight coil to the soldiers while we tried to save Donald. My Senior Medic and First Sergeant were climbing into the turret immediately to pull Donald out while the rest of the soldiers strengthened the defenses. The entire company had arrived in a few minutes and we were able to evacuate Donald quickly, but there was nothing anyone could do for him. He was already gone.

By the time Donald was evacuated, I already had the Company advancing to make contact with the men who fired the RPG's. They behaved as they always do and ran as far and as fast as they could. It became apparent very quickly that we were not going to be able to make direct fire contact with the enemy and kill him because he had run away and hid among the populace. We questioned the Iraqi's present during the ambush but they refused to tell Americans anything. We decided to pull back and send in our informants, who are Iraqi citizens friendly to the U.S. These men were able to quickly find someone who saw the faces of the men that fired the RPG's. The informant also knew where one of them lived. This information came in at about 10pm on the 13th.

I quickly issued an order for 1st Platoon to conduct a raid on this target. At 1am on 14th of October, the 1st Platoon assaulted the target house. The house had seven women and one man in it. The man turned out to be the father of the suspect. We arrested him. I put the house under observation, and it is still under observation as I write this. Our informants later found that the suspect had moved out of his house by the 10th of October and was living with the Fedayeen. We still have the father in custody and we have since captured one of the suspect's friends. Unfortunately, we have not located the suspects yet. Please know that we are doing everything we can to find these men and capture or kill them. The entire Battalion is focused on bringing these men to justice.

I know words cannot begin to ease the pain of your loss, but please know that Donald gave his life protecting his friends and his unit. Donald's actions while providing rear security for his section prevented the loss of other soldiers. Everyone in Charlie Company is keenly aware of his and your sacrifice for all of us. I am at your service if you need any assistance. If there are any questions you need answered or any service you need and you think Charlie Company can help, please let me know. Every soldier here will be eager to do whatever they can for you. God Bless You.

I had to respond to Captain Boyd's kindness. The grueling task of reliving DJ's last day was a handwritten letter four pages long while he still was deployed. I knew from DJ's own words they had little to no time for themselves but yet Captain Boyd found the time to relive the death of his fellow comrade. All because his compassion and love for us, DJ's family, outweighed his own rest and comfort. But I knew, all to well, that he was the one still in harm's way. He had to put on his boots and helmet and pick up his weapon and continue putting his life on the line for me, an American Citizen. I needed him to know I cared for him and I desperately wanted him to return safely to his family. I mailed the following on November 24, 2003.

Dear Captain Brad Boyd,

I'm Mary Cay Wheeler, SPC Donald L. Wheeler, Jr.'s Mom. I thank you for taking time to write to us about the day, **October 13, 2003**. I realize you have little to no time off and to spend that time recalling a "difficult" day means so much. Facts and words telling about the life DJ and all of you live, day in and day out, helps to fill in the emptiness. I am envious of where you are. I want to be there. I want to fight. I want to help eradicate the evil To sit here and try to go about living as if all is okay is crazy. Nothing will be "normal" again. My faith tells me my prayers are powerful. My heart and soul never leaves the Throne Room of God. Good will triumphant over evil. I also know my son, DJ, he will not leave his comrades. He will, due to God's Grace and Mercy, help all of you with his new body. His spirit will remain close to you. DJ is still in the fight. His blood cries out from the ground in Tikrit. Justice will be had.

Please let everyone know that DJ's family is stronger than ever and the prayers of our Nation are behind you. A powerful prayer that DJ wrote home saying, *"It is the only way to stay sane"* **is the rosary.** I am including it in a package that William Velez will be receiving. I pray that by meditating on Jesus' life will bring peace to your heart and clear thinking to your mind so God will be able to continue to guide and protect you from the enemies of peace.

Again, Brad, don't fret about DJ's family. Stay focused and keep God as your center so with every footstep you take evil retreats and all of America says AMEN, AMEN, AMEN.

COME HOLY SPIRIT. A powerful short prayer. Use it.

God Bless you, Brad.

Following is a posting from DJ's battalion commander, LTC Steven D. Russell entitled "Reflections of October 13, 2003" posted at the battalion website: http://1-22infantry.org/current/updatedec25.htm

We continued our operations in Tikrit the next day, conducting our bomb sweeps along the main roads and those that connect them. C Company had primary responsibility for the built up area of the city. In the afternoon, 1st Platoon patrolled with Bradleys and Infantry in the part of the city we call the 'chevron,' because on the map, it makes a pointed shape at the northern third of the city. 1LT Jason Price was leading a two-vehicle section along the street parallel to the mosque with the soccer field. They turned right, heading east toward Highway 1 and the 'Lucky Panda' ice cream shop, continuing to look for bombs along the curbs.

SSG Bordes in the trail Bradley had his turret turned to the rear to provide 360 degree security. He looked forward as the vehicle travels while his gunner, standing up to provide additional eyes for the bomb threat, looked toward the rear. A short distance after they made the turn, SSG Bordes blacked out. He came to in a daze, realizing something was wrong. He saw his driver was OK after talking to him and could see his **gunner** standing next to him. He stood back up to make sure he was OK as well and noticed that he was laying back against the hatch, his helmet gone. The shoe-box sized Integrated Site Unit (ISU) in front of him was blown apart and pushed against him as well. SSG Michael Bordes called for a medevac and attempted to render what aid he could. No aid could be rendered. His **gunner** slumped into the turret, already dead.

1LT Price called the medevac and his crews did what they could while also pulling security. The vehicle was hit by an RPG, which penetrated the ISU. We determined that two men had fired a volley of RPGs from a blind corner in the built up housing area. As the **gunner** was the one looking to the rear, he was the only one that could have seen where the shot came from that killed him. CPT Brad Boyd arrived at the scene and they cleared the area looking for the attackers. 1SG Michael Evans, SSG Felipe Madrid and SSG Bordes eased the **gunner** out of the turret and onto a stretcher. CPT Jason Deel with the civil defense troops took him to our battalion aid station. I received the news coming out of a meeting with local officials and rushed to the scene. There was nothing I could do. The Bradley was not damaged except for its sight and 1st Platoon took it back to the company's compound. I called for a fire truck to wash down the streets. I wanted no visible traces of anything for the enemy to gloat over. We took our losses and cracked down on the city, looking for the perpetrators. Locals provided some useful information and a manhunt netted partial results over the next couple of days. The soldiers of the 1st Battalion, 22nd Infantry and some from 3rd Battalion, 66th Armor gathered at Saddam's Birthday Palace on the 15th. The Bears of B Company and Cobras of C Company stood on that same asphalt used for Saddam's military parades. A chaplain stepped forward and prayed. Purple Hearts and Bronze Star Medals for making the ultimate sacrifice were laid on pairs of boots overshadowed by lone rifles with Kevlar helmets planted on top. At a podium, commanders and friends struggled to find words that vocabularies failed to adequately provide. Soldiers stood at attention. Specialist James Edward Powell's name rang out for roll call in B Company. He did not answer. Neither did Specialist Donald Laverne Wheeler, Jr. of C Company. Taps resonated in mournful tones. Tears rolled down faces as we remembered their lives. Rifle shots cracked in three sharp volleys, interrupting these reflections—a startling reminder of the price of our freedom.

CHAPTER SIX: LAYING TO REST

Details come from three DVD's compiled by relatives to honor DJ.

TUESDAY, OCTOBER 21, 2003

MASS OF CHRISTIAN BURIAL

PROGRAM: **QUEEN OF THE MIRACULOUS MEDAL CATHOLIC CHURCH in JACKSON, MICHIGAN**

OPENING HYMN On Eagle's Wings
INTRODUCTORY RITES Greeting; Sprinkling with Holy Water; Placing of the Pall;
Opening Prayer: Lord God source and destiny of our lives in Your loving providence You gave us DJ to grow in wisdom, age, and grace. Now You have called him to Yourself. As we grieve over the loss of one so young, we seek to understand Your purpose. Draw him to Yourself and give him full stature in Christ. May he stand with all the Angels and Saints who know Your love and praise Your saving will. We ask this through Christ our Lord. **Amen.**

LITURGY OF THE WORD

First Reading read by Phyllis Wheeler   Ecclesiastes 3:1-11

There is an appointed time for everything, and a time for every affair under the heavens: A time to be born, and a time to die; a time to plant, and a time to uproot the plant. A time to kill, and a time to heal; a time to tear down, and a time to build. A time to weep, and a time to laugh; a time to mourn, and a time to dance. A time to scatter stones, and a time to gather them; a time to embrace, and a time to be far from embraces. A time to seek, and a time to lose; a time to keep, and a time to cast away. A time to rend, and a time to sew; a time to be silent, and a time to speak. A time to love, and a time to hate; a time of war, and a time of peace.

What advantage has the worker from his toil? I have considered the task, which God has appointed for men to be busied about. He has made everything appropriate to its time, and has put the timeless into their hearts, without men ever discovering, from beginning to end, the work which God has done.

The Word of the Lord.   ***Thanks be to God.***
Response: *"Be with me Lord when I am in trouble, be with me Lord I pray."*

Second Reading read by Bernadette Wheeler Romans 8:31-35, 37-39

If God is for us, who can be against us? Is it possible that He Who did not spare His Own Son but handed Him over for the sake of us all will not grant us all things besides? Who shall bring a charge against God's chosen ones? God, Who justifies? Who shall condemn them? Christ Jesus, Who died or rather was raised up, Who is at the right Hand of God and Who intercedes for us?

Who will separate us from the love of Christ? Trial, or distress, or persecution, or hunger, or nakedness, or danger, or the sword? Yet in all this we are more than conquerors because of Him Who has loved us. For I am certain that neither death nor life, neither Angels nor principalities, neither the present nor the future, nor powers, neither height nor depth nor any other creature, will be able to separate us from the love of God that comes to us in Christ Jesus, our Lord.

The Word of the Lord.   ***Thanks be to God.***

Gospel   John 12:23-28

Jesus told His disciples:

"The Hour has come for the Son of Man to be glorified. Amen, amen, I say to you, unless a grain of wheat falls to the ground and dies, it remains just a grain of wheat; but if it dies, it produces much fruit. Whoever loves his life loses it, and whoever hates his life in this world will preserve it for eternal life. Whoever serves Me must follow Me, and where I am, there also will My servant be. The Father will honor whoever serves Me. I am troubled now. Yet what should I say? 'Father, save Me from this Hour?' But it was for this purpose that I came to this Hour. Father Glorify Your Name."

The Voice came down from Heaven, *"I have glorified It and will glorify It again."*

The Gospel of the Lord   ***Praise to You, Lord Jesus Christ***

Homily by our pastor, Father Thomas Nenneau:

Indeed as I begin let us proclaim a litany of saints with Marycay and Don, Andrea, Phyllis, and Bernadette. Burt, Trevor, Thomas, Quentin, Paul, Spencer, Dominic, Patrick. And to DJ's grandparents, all his relatives, all his cousins, friends gathered here today. My own feeling of sincere sympathy and loss at this time. As DJ's pastor, this is certainly an occasion that few priests want to encounter. I express my own sympathy and regrets. I also include the entire parish family. Many are here with us today through our Arimatheans *(parishioners who help at funerals)* and parishioners from Saint Joseph's and their Arimatheans and all the priests that are gathered here today throughout the area to show their love and prayerful support.

As a Navy Chaplain since 1984, I have been assigned to many sailors and marines. I have had the sad duty of casualty calls to inform the parents and loved ones that their son, daughter, or spouse has been taken from them. But in all that time never did I have anyone killed in a War from a parish that was entrusted to me as pastor. And as I think about those realities, I recall that day, November 3rd in 2001, when I drove to the Wheeler home in Concord to partake in a little prayer and blessing service for DJ as he prepared to leave for his basic training. On that day we prayed the rosary and after the rosary was done I gave my prayer of blessing as DJ held down his head. I laid my hand on top of his head and I prayed a prayer. I cannot remember all the details of the prayer because I prayed them from my heart. But I recall that what I did pray were three things for DJ:

That he be kept from harm's way.

I prayed that if he did get in harm's way that he would be saved.

I prayed he be a good soldier.

He was not kept from harm's way. And when in harm's way, neither, was he kept safe. But he was a good soldier.

He was a good soldier. He was a good soldier because he was a man of commitment. I mention that because I gave that blessing a day or two before he left for basic training. November 3rd of 2001. That was less than two months after the cruel act upon our country. As you have probably read or heard from a newspaper article or television, after that attack DJ said that he needed to do something to help fight this evil. So DJ was a good soldier because he was a man of commitment. He did not say, *"What can I do in the face of this evil that will make me happy, that will keep me safe, that will keep me out of trouble."* Nowadays you can read about the crisis of commitment we have in our nation. People who don't know how to be committed. They are only concerned about those things that will make themselves happy.

DJ was a good soldier because he was a man of commitment. He did not do those things that would simply please himself. But he was willing to do things for others. He, like any good soldier, sailor, marine or airman, accept principles greater than himself. Not only accept those principles but was even willing to put his life on the line for something greater than himself - for the principles and the values that we hold so dear as American people. DJ was a good soldier because he was a man of commitment.

He was a good soldier because he was a good comrade. We have read so much and heard so much about his infectious smile. About his happy and good disposition. About the joy that he brought to others. It was not something he simply did here in Jackson. That was not just something he did here at our parish or at Lumen Christi or JCMS or other places he went to school. No. It was something he did as a soldier. I have heard of the tributes that have come in about DJ since his death, about the way his infectious smile affected his fellow soldiers and comrades. About how he would lift up their spirits to make them happy. Here they are as far away from home as he was but he used his own personality, his own goodness, his own joyfulness, to lift them up. He only knew them for a short time but soldiers were already referring to him as their best friend. That is a *good* soldier because he was a good comrade. And it is true, that in only a few moments before he went out to the Bradley that he was with one of his brother soldier and as one can expect, they were laughing and joking around - being good to one another. As they parted that was the patrol that he was (*emotional*)...when he was killed. Moments before his death he was showing himself to be a good soldier because he was a good comrade.

He was also a good soldier because as the opening prayer mentioned, he was seeking to grow to full stature in Christ. It was no surprise, knowing the Wheeler family, that DJ left here for basic training with the rosary and a Bible and a religious medal. And these were not things that he put in his duffel bag or put into a drawer and said, *"Thanks, Mom and Dad"* and forgot about them. No. They were things that he treasured. A letter that he wrote back testifying these were things that he was using. He was using them to help his Faith to grow to full stature in Christ. My own most personal, most treasured possession is this, The New Testament that was given to my Father when he was commissioned as an officer in the Army Air Force during the Second World War as a flight instructor. I keep this Bible because it is a sign and symbol of his commitment to principles and values that were greater than himself. It is his sign of his willingness to live for values that we all might be able to enjoy in our own lives. Even my Dad was seeking in his life to grow to the full stature in Christ. And I have It to honor him. I honor him for the last many years by wearing a replica of the religious medal that was given to him and all Catholic service men and women of the Second World War. I honor him in that way as he sought to grow in the full stature in Christ. We honor DJ, too, because he used those things so he could grow in full stature while at war as a Christian gentleman, indeed as a Christian soldier.

We have heard in Holy Scriptures today these words from our Lord Jesus as His Death gets closer, *"What am I supposed to say? Save Me from this hour? It was for this Hour that I came."* Soldiers, sailors, marines, airmen, DJ. They understand these words. When one is called to Duty – when one is called to that which they have committed their life to do, they do it. They do it willingly because it is part of their character that they have taken upon themselves. Part of their character that they have become.

Saint Paul here says in the Letter to the Romans, *"Who will separate us from the Love of Christ?"* Will DJ's death separate him from the Love of Christ? Will his death separate him from our love? From our admiration and our esteem? If you don't believe in eternal life, then yes it will, because it is the wrong choice. But as Christians we *know* nothing will separate us from the Love of Christ unless we allow it to do so ourselves. DJ was not going to allow it to happen to him. By the example of his mom and dad, the example of his grandparents, his brothers and sisters who supported him, he would grow indeed to full stature in Christ. And he has left us as a Christian gentleman. He has left us as a Christian soldier.

The Army has a very simple but yet very profound practice when a soldier is lost. I saw it in the newspaper the other day. They gather in companies and they call out the names. *"SPC Donald Wheeler, Jr."* was called out there in Iraq. There was no answer. They called it a second time: *"SPC Donald L Wheeler, Jr."* The second time. No answer. *"SPC Donald Wheeler, Jr."* called for one last time, the third time. Once again there was no answer. So at that third time his name is enrolled in the list of the Fallen.

But at the same time, however, in the Heavenly Host, there was another roll call taking place in Heaven. And the Lord Jesus was there and He said, *"SPC Donald L Wheeler, Jr., DJ, Don."* and among the Heavenly Host, DJ responded, *"Present. Here I am, Lord."*

General Intercessions read by Andrea Wheeler Barrett.
LITURGY OF THE EUCHARIST
Offertory Hymn: "Amazing Grace"; Presentation of the Gifts by family members; Eucharistic Prayer; The Lord's Prayer; Sign of Peace; Communion Meditation Song: "Ave Maria"; Song of Thanksgiving: "Bread of Life"; Reflection Song: "Surely the Presence"

Poem written by Bernadette Wheeler,
read by Andrea (Wheeler) Barrett
My brother died today
the pain won't ever fade.
I pray to God he's in a state of peace,
the memories of him will never cease.
He was more than just a brother, he was my best friend,
who cared so much about me and my family without extent.
I keep telling myself he's still fighting the war in Iraq.
I keep wishing and praying with all my heart
that he'll come back.
To squeeze my neck and give me those big hugs,
and tell me that I am someone whom he loves.
But then I remember that soldier guy,
he was so compassionate and so very kind,
he told me that DJ had just died.

73

I cried, then cried, and cried.
I remember all those funny jokes and that charming smile.
All of these things I will not see for a while.
That famous wink, and crazy hair,
Dear Lord God, I wish he was here.
Those loving words he would speak,
All of these recalled make me weak.
I just hope, I just pray
that when the time comes
I'll see my brother again someday.
But DJ will never be dead to me.
I'll keep him alive in my memory.
He's in a greater place now, up above.
He's probably chilling with all the ones whom he loved.
But Lord, while You have him please keep in mind,
that person that You took was one of a kind.
No one else could lighten up your day
like DJ could by simply saying, "Hey."
And Lord most of all, please don't let anyone ever forget,
That brave young soldier who gave his life for us, without regret.

Reflections by Mary Catherine Wheeler

A grain of wheat must fall to the ground and die or it remains just a grain of wheat. God did not spare His own Son but handed him over and nothing will separate us from the love of God. There is an appointed time for everything, a time for every affair under the heavens. There is a time to be born, and a time to die.

October 13th, 2003, the time for our son, Donald Laverne Wheeler, Jr., to give the ultimate gift for what he believed.

October 13th, 2003. Donald Laverne Wheeler, Jr.'s last day on earth but his first day in Eternal Life.

October 13th is also the anniversary of the last appearance of Blessed Mary at Fatima, where She was asking us to pray the rosary and for the urgency of penance and for conversion and to have faith. DJ was living that message, Praying the rosary, urgently doing penance, and being open to change. He had total faith and trust in God as he served under hardships we can only imagine. He remained hope-filled and cheerful, as it has been testified by men that had the privilege to serve with him. God is ever faithful and true. He called our son and our son answered that call. I want DJ's own words to be heard. For he has something to tell us.

"I pray for you all every day by saying the rosary. It's the only way to stay sane out here with all that's happened so far and still to happen. My family, my inspiration, for dad and mom, all the way down to Patrick. Everyone unique in their own way. When it gets hard to deal with this

place I pray for all of you. Each one in their own battles in life...to some of yours, make this seem easy. But be strong. It'll all work out in the end."

Do you hear him? Do you hear DJ? How he found peace in the midst of hell was with Blessed Mary, the Mother of God whom God has Her called the Queen of Peace. He was able to excel due to his ability to find that peace. Living out his commitment to the United States of America. He, truly, found his calling. Where God needed him. I gave our son to Blessed Mary when we parted. Asking Her to hold him for me until I could do it again. Our heavenly Mother cradled DJ under Her motherly Mantle of Peace and led him to God. As our First Reading said, there is an appointed time for everything and a time for every affair under the heavens. When we said goodbye to DJ, that was the time for an embrace, and this is the time to be far from embracing.

The Second Reading He did not spare His own Son but handed Him over. Our son has been handed over. But never are we separated from him or the love of God through Christ Jesus our Lord.

From the Gospel, the grain of wheat was DJ. He was broken open and his blood fell into the ground in Tikrit and the fruits of that sacrifice are beginning to unfold and produce fruit that will last. I must confess I might begin to feel abandoned by God but I hold on to His Word. He is Truth. And my response to that is, "Jesus, I Trust in You." It will be my commitment to DJ to help *his* message to our family be shared with the world.

More of DJ's words are: *"Someone is watching over us over here. I can feel HIM."* God is ever faithful and true. He did not abandon our son. People have said to me, *"Your poor family. You have been through so much."* Some may feel we are being punished by God for some past wrongs or present wrongs. I submit to you, God is saying watch this family as they carry their cross. Their faith does not waiver. People make choices in life. In DJ's case a lunatic decided to run from an alleyway and shoot an RPG at my son's Bradley. Evil was chosen and bad things happened. But good will prevail.

God gave me a message the day we received the news of DJ's heroic act. I want to share that with all of you now.

DJ chose Saint Michael, the Archangel, as his confirmation name so in the prayer that we say to Saint Michael, we have *always* connected it to DJ. And since he joined the Army, we were always hope-filled that God would allow Saint Michael to take care of him. The news of DJ's sacrifice was brought to us by SGT Johnson. I asked him his first name. He hesitated but then said it was Michael. It made me smile and feel happy, even in that horrible hour. God was letting me know, we sent DJ with Saint Michael to watch over him and here is Michael telling us he was with God. Saint Michael is with him still, and their work is not done.

Some may say God didn't answer your prayers. He didn't care for your son. DJ's gone. But I submit to you He did. A grain of wheat must die. God's own Son was not spared. Evil shortened DJ's life and God is letting me know to continue to trust Him and listen to Blessed Mary, the Queen of Peace, and He will turn what looks like a disaster into a blessing. The Crucifixion looked like a disaster to the disciples but they needed to keep on believing. God is saying,

"Remember Saint Peter Who was able to walk on turbulent waters – as will you walk through this as long as you keep your eyes on Me."

We will continue to trust God. *For where would we go?* We will hold up under the weight of this cross. Our faith in God will not waiver. Remember DJ's own words, *"It'll all work out in the end."*

There is where our hope lies. That is where we place our Trust. Trusting God that it will all work out in the end. So just like Saint Simon while under the weight of the cross, we will turn our head and we will see the Face of God.

October the 13th, a time for Donald Laverne Wheeler, Jr.'s birth into Eternal Life.

October the 13th, a Time to commit to pray more, to be open to change and to do penance to obtain Peace in our world.

I love you, DJ. Thank you for the privilege of being your Mom.

CONCLUDING RITES

Prayer; Signs of Farewell; Prayer of Commendation: *"Receive his soul and present him to God the Most High"*; Closing Hymn: "America the Beautiful".

Pall Bearers	Honorary Pall Bearers
Burt Wheeler	Henry Thorrez
Trevor Wheeler	John Thorrez
Wes Stevens	Christopher Thorrez
Thomas Wheeler	Nicholas Thorrez
Quentin Wheeler	Matthew Thorrez
Paul Wheeler	Peter Thorrez
Spencer Wheeler	Donald Hershberger
Dominic Wheeler	Mark Palmer
Patrick Wheeler	Jacob Barrett

*   *   *   *   *

As we processed from the church to the cemetery, the streets were lined with people holding Flags and saluting. When we were going past DJ's high school, all the students were standing in attentive respect.

76

My Dear Parents,   November 10, 2003
   (We had an event that) had to do with Donald L. Wheeler, Jr.'s funeral. Approximately 200 Lumen Christi students attended the funeral. Father Tom Nenneau's homily and the eulogy delivered by DJ's mother were profound examples of how people of faith handle sudden and tragic death. I was so happy that so many of our youth heard the talks and took the messages to heart. The funeral procession drove by Lumen Christi. The rest of the student body, 440 teenagers, lined Spring Arbor Road quietly and prayerfully while the cortege drove by. Viewing so many family and friends so sad over a life of potential cut short, our students showed visibly how deeply they were affected by the passing of this brave soldier. They returned to the building in a somber and quiet state. This event proved to me once again that if we expect great things of our youth; more than likely they will measure up and sometimes surpass our expectations.
   "Jesus' power working in us enables us to do so much more
   than we can ever ask for or even think of"(Eph 3:20).

   Those who joined us at the cemetery did so under skies that were gray and threatening rain and the sound of a band playing our national anthem. "The Star-Spangled Banner" was greatly appreciated. The history of this song goes back to 1889 when the Secretary of the Navy signed an order making it the tune to be played whenever the Flag was raised. Then it became the official tune to be played at all military occasions, ordered by President Woodrow Wilson in 1916. A real tribute to the stars on our Flag in keeping with DJ's memory, *"Shine on the world like bright stars you are offering it the Word of Life"* (Phil 2:15) and *"one day the Flag will honor you, DJ"*. The lyrics are beautiful. Here are a few lines.
   ...Gave proof through the night that our Flag was still there;
   O say does that star-spangled banner yet wave,
   O'er the land of the free and the home of the brave?...

   ...Praise the Power that hath made and preserved us a nation!
   Then conquer we must, when our cause it is just,
   And this be our motto: *"In God is our Trust."*
   And the star-spangled banner in triumph shall wave
   O'er the land of the free and the home of the brave!

THE RITE OF COMMITTAL Father Nenneau, dressed in his Navy
                                         Chaplain Uniform:

Our brother DJ has gone to his rest in the Peace of Christ and may the Lord now welcome him to the table of God's children in Heaven. With Faith and Hope in Eternal Life let us also assist him with our prayers. Let us pray to the Lord for ourselves as well. May we who mourn be reunited one day with our brother and together may we meet Christ Jesus when He, Who is our life, appears in His Glory.

BLESSING OF THE GRAVE

We read in Sacred Scriptures the 6th Chapter of the Gospel of Saint John 39th verse, *"This is the will of the One who sent Me, says the Lord, that I should not lose anything of what He gave Me but that I shall raise it up on the last day."*

Lord Jesus Christ, by Your Own three days in the tomb You hallowed the graves of all who believe in You and so made the grave a sign of hope that promises Resurrection even as it claims our mortal bodies. Grant that our brother may sleep here in peace until You awaken him into Glory where You are the Resurrection and the Life. Then he will see You face to Face and in Your Light and he will see light and know the splendor of God where You live and reign forever and ever.

Amen.

THE COMMITTAL

Because God has chosen to call our brother from this life to Himself we commit his body to the earth for we are dust and unto dust we shall return. But the Lord Jesus Christ will change our mortal bodies to be like His Own in glory, for He is risen and He is the first born from the dead. Let us therefore commend our brother to the Lord and that He will embrace him in peace and raise up his body on the last day.

INTERCESSIONS

We pray for DJ to our Lord Jesus Christ, Who said, "I am the Resurrection and the Life. Whoever believes in Me shall live even in death. And whoever believes in Me shall never suffer eternal death."

Lord, You consoled Martha and Mary in their distress. Draw near to us who mourn and dry the tears of those who weep. We pray to the Lord.

Lord hear our prayer.

You wept at the grave of Lazarus, Your friend. Comfort us in our sorrow. We pray to the Lord.

Lord hear our prayer

You raised the dead to life. Give to our brother Eternal Life. We pray to the Lord.

Lord hear our prayer.

DJ was washed in Baptism and anointed with the Holy Spirit. Give him fellowship with all Your Saints. We pray to the Lord.

Lord hear our prayer.

He was nourished with Your Body and Blood. Grant him a place at the Table in Your heavenly Kingdom. We pray to the Lord.

Lord hear our prayer.

Comfort us in our sorrow at his death. May our faith be our consolation and Eternal Life be our hope. We pray to the Lord.

Lord hear our prayer.

Longing for the coming of God's kingdom we pray as our Lord Jesus taught us. **OUR FATHER....**

Oh Mighty God, through the Death of Your Son on the Cross, You destroyed our death through His rest in the tomb. You hallowed the graves for all who believe in You and through His rising again You restored us to Eternal Life. God of the Living and the Dead, accept our prayers for those who have died in Christ and are buried with Him in the hope of rising again. Since they were true to Your Name on earth let them praise You forever in the joy of Heaven. We ask this through Christ our Lord.

Amen.

PRAYER OVER THE PEOPLE

Merciful Lord, You know the anguish of the sorrowful and You are attentive to the prayers of the humble. Hear Your people who cry out to You in their need and strengthen their hope in Your lasting goodness.

Eternal rest grant unto him, O Lord

And let perpetual Light shine upon him

And may he rest in peace

Amen.

May his soul and the souls of all the faithfully departed through the mercy of God, rest in peace.

Amen.

And may the peace of God which surpasses all human understanding keep our hearts and our minds in the knowledge and the love of God and of His Son, our Lord and Savior, Jesus Christ.

Amen.

If we could all now please join in singing the "Battle Hymn of The Republic."

Mine eyes have seen the glory of the coming of the Lord:
He is trampling out the vintage where the grapes of wrath are stored;
He hath loosed the fateful lightning of His terrible swift sword:
His Truth is marching on.

Refrain:
Glory, glory, hallelujah!
Glory, glory, hallelujah!
Glory, glory, hallelujah!
His Truth is marching on.

In the beauty of the lilies Christ was born across the sea,
With a glory in His bosom that transfigures you and me:
As He died to make us holy, let us die that all be free,
While God is marching on. **Refrain:**
He is coming like the glory of the morning on the wave,
He is Wisdom to the mighty, He is honor to the brave,
So the world shall be His footstool, and the evil power his slave.
Our God is marching on. **Refrain:**

PRESENTATION OF THE MEDALS by Escort Officer (EO)
CPT Matthew Weber

The President of the United States of America has awarded the Bronze Star Medal to SPC Donald L. Wheeler, Jr for meritorious service from 19th March of 2003 to 13th October, 2003, while assigned to Company C 1st Battalion 22nd Infantry Regiment, 4th Infantry Division. SPC Wheeler gave the ultimate sacrifice while participating in combat operations to liberate Iraq. His duty performance and commitment are keeping with the highest traditions of self-less service and reflects great credit upon himself and the 4th Infantry Division and the U.S. Army. Given under my hand in the city of Washington this 15th day of October, 2003. Signed R. L. Brownlee, Secretary of the Army.

The President of the United States of America has award the Purple Heart to SPC Donald L. Wheeler, Jr. for wounds received in Action on 13th October, 2003 given under my hand in the city of Washington this 14th day of October 2003. Signed R.L. Brownlee, Secretary of the Army.

SPC Donald L Wheeler, Jr. is awarded the Combat Infantryman's Badge for performance of duty while under hostile fire. By order of the Secretary of the Army.

21-GUN SALUTE Peaceful intentions. Seven men shooting three rifle volleys. Seven; God rested on the seventh day; with volleys of three – an old battlefield tradition signaling it was time to care for the wounded and the dead.

TAPS BY LONE BUGLER Up to the Civil War a French tune was played called *Lights Out* but after a battle leaving 600 men dead and wounded, Union Army Gen. Butterfield changed the notes with the intent to honor the men.

FLAG FOLDING One of the seven soldiers who did the 21-gun salute remained in position, called Parade Rest, while the other six placed three rifles in two triangular shapes called Stack Arms, and march to the grave site. Once there, they organized themselves to form two lines of three, facing each other and separated by five feet. Slowly the two closest to DJ removed the Flag and commenced to do the formal, precision folding. When it is completed, three empty shell casings from the 21-gun salute, symbolizing duty, honor, and country, are put into the fold of the Flag. Seven minutes later It is placed in my arms as these words are spoken:

"This Flag is presented to you on behalf of a grateful Nation and the United States Army as a token of appreciation for your loved one's honorable and faithful service."

I sat back down. I had accepted the Flag for the last time. The first time it was put into my hands back at the funeral home. Then as I was processing behind the coffin, flanked by my eight sons into church - I held it close. At the end of the service I gave the Flag back so It could honor DJ for his last ride from Jackson to Concord, a drive DJ had driven countless times. Now the Flag was in my possession forever. It was the only tangible item that connected me to *most* of the places DJ had been since I hugged him goodbye at Fort Hood, Texas. It went places where I was not allowed to go. That is why It is very sacred to me. At the grave site, a military man told me he had never seen the folding done with such care. I knew it was evidence of God's Mighty Hand. I have since learned more about the folding of the Flag.

There are 13 folds – 13 is another connection to Our Lady of Fatima, the Mother of God.

The triangle shape represents the three corner hats worn when our nation fought for Independence from England – a hat worn proclaims who we are. "Tri" means three; three points in one with my intent to symbolize The Trinity: Father, Son, and Holy Spirit. We are a Nation under God – whom we love, honor, and humbly receive our strength.

The 13th side faces up and displays white stars on the blue background – the blue for Blessed Mary. The stars – DJ's 4th religion class: *"Shine on the world like bright stars you are offering It the Word of Life."* The Light of Christ to shine on our Nation and the world.

The Flag consists of 13 horizontal stripes, seven red alternating with six white. The stripes represent the original 13 colonies; the stars represent the 50 states of the Union. The colors of the Flag were chosen with the intent to symbolize:

Red - Hardiness and Valor

White - Purity and Innocence

Blue - Vigilance, Perseverance and Justice

ANNOUNCEMENT: *"This concludes the services."*

Even as I review these DVDs that were compiled in honor of DJ, it still seems unbelievable. But it is the Truth and Truth is necessary to carry-on.

"YOUR CROSS"

"THE EVERLASTING GOD has, in His wisdom, foreseen from eternity the cross that He now presents to you as a Gift from His inmost Heart. This cross He now sends you He has considered with His all-knowing Eyes, understood with His Divine Mind, tested with His wise Justice, warmed with His loving Arms and weighted with His own Hands to see that It be not one inch too large and not one ounce too heavy for you. He has blessed it with His holy Name, anointed it with His Grace, perfumed it with His Consolation, taken one last glance at you and your courage, and then sent it to you from Heaven, a special greeting from God to you and an alms of the all-merciful Love of God."

(Saint Francis de Sales Doctor of the Church-Thank you, Fr Helfrich)

To deny the Truth would be to deny the Cross; the Gift from God. To accept this Gift will add depth to your life and greater love for God. Do not reach for something or someone to divert your attention away from God. Take the time to go deep within yourself and discover just how close God is to you.

"He will never leave you or forsake you"(Deut 31:6).

This is His Promise, so persevere in hope and faith.

"The One Who promises never fails"(Luke 1:37).

If you doubt His Word then you give the enemy a foothold in your life. Denial, guilt, anger, impatience, indifference, depression are warning signs. These could be directed to yourself, spouse, family, friends, God – to everyone. The choice is yours. But be aware you are setting yourself up for more pain and heartache. So listen to this good advice:

"Have patience with all things, but chiefly have patience with yourself.
Do not lose courage... every day begin anew" (Saint Francis de Sales).

Helpful suggestions: Stop asking, *"Why?"* Go to daily Mass. Go to Reconciliation at least monthly. Go to church to sit with God and tell Him honestly what you are feeling. *Listen.* Read a chapter a day from the four gospels to hear His Word. *Be still.* Pray, pray, pray. *Listen.* Be open to His Gift of Grace which allows His Love, Peace and Joy to flow into you.

"My thoughts are not your thoughts, nor are your ways My ways"(Is 55:8).

Remember God loves you more than anyone on earth or in Heaven could possibly love you.

"For God so loved the world, that He gave His only Son, that whoever believes in Him should not perish but have Eternal Life" (John 3:16).

I discovered a beautiful song at the beginning of my struggle written and performed by Babbie Mason. The lyrics are biblically sound, starting with Romans 8:28 *"All things work for our good"* and *"His Ways are not our own"* Isaiah 55:8. So strive to shine in our world as *you* offer it the Word of Life.

"Trust His Heart"

All things work for our good,
though sometimes we don't see how they could,
Struggles that break our hearts in two, Sometimes blind us to the truth,
Our Father knows what's best for us, His ways are not our own,
So when your pathway grows dim, and you just don't see Him,
Remember you're never alone

REFRAIN: *God is too wise to be mistaken*
God is too good to be unkind
So when you don't understand
When you don't see His Plan
When you can't trace His Hand
Trust His heart
Trust His heart

He sees the Master Plan, And He holds our future in His Hand,
So don't live as those who have no hope,
All our hope is found in Him,
We see the present clearly, But He sees the first and the last,
And like a tapestry, He's weaving you and me,
To someday be just like Him – He alone is faithful and true,
He alone knows what is best for you.

REFRAIN:

The grave. So final. So grim. But I remember Saint Paul's words:
"O death, where is your victory? O death where is your sting"(Cor 15:55). So it is not the end or final. I also choose to listen to DJ's words when he wrote:

"It'll all work out in the end."

DJ reminds us not to give up. We are a hopeful people because of The Paschal Mystery; The Last Supper; Sacrifice of the Cross – suffering and dying; and His Resurrection, rising from the dead. My Trust remains in Him.

"Father, because Jesus, Your Servant, became obedient even unto death, His Sacrifice was greater than all holocausts of old. Accept the sacrifice of praise we offer You through Him, and may we show the effects

of It in our lives by striving to do Your Will until our whole life becomes adoration in spirit and truth"(Div Off Vol IV pg 1217).

With the service officially over, the people that were so lovingly generous by joining our family, now amazed me further by forming a line. They took turns paying their respects to DJ and at the same time giving me a hug. Since I still had the Flag in my arms, unbeknownst to them, they were thanking the Flag that never left SPC Donald L. Wheeler, Jr. when he left Iraq to go to Germany to Delaware to Michigan. The very Flag that I had told DJ back in June, 2002 would one day honor him. Their embrace embedded their love into DJ's Flag, honored him! This will be forever in my memory, words fail to convey how much it means to me.

TIKRIT PALACE COMPLEX, IRAQ
LTC Steven D. Russell, Infantry

Dear Mr and Mrs Wheeler,   14 October 2003

I cannot begin to tell you how grieved we are at the loss of your son Donald, Jr. I participated on many combat operations with him and found him to be nothing but an outstanding soldier. I was proud to be his battalion commander. He took great pride in his efficiency with the weapons on his Bradley Fighting Vehicle and was a proficient gunner. He was a very good soldier.

Don died yesterday defending his fellow soldiers from 1st Platoon, C Company on a combat patrol heading north on a side street in Tikrit, Iraq. He was on the trail Bradley in a two armored vehicle patrol. As they turned east onto a connecting street to the main highway, Don and the Bradley commander were scanning to the rear to protect from any enemy that may be behind them. An enemy element fired into the turret and the explosion killed him instantly. He did not suffer and it is likely he never saw the fire that hit him.

Don was a popular soldier. Our men were greatly shaken by his loss and we still cannot believe he is gone. Words cannot express how much our hearts go out to you and your family. We feel he was part of our family in a sense as well and his loss is like losing a brother.

I wish there was something I could say or offer to you but I cannot think of what could possibly matter. But I wanted to say how deeply moved all of his fellow soldiers were when we lost him. Our hearts go out to you and your family in this time of mourning. If you have any questions or if there is something we could ever do concerning Don, please let us know. I am very sorry for his loss.

SFC Kelly W. Lucas, Platoon Sergeant

Dear Mr. and Mrs. Wheeler and Family,   4 December 2003
    I am writing this letter in deepest regret for the loss of your son/brother. I have just recently returned from Iraq and this is the first opportunity I have had to contact you. I was Specialist Wheeler's Platoon Sergeant while he was with 2nd Platoon, Charlie Company, 1-22 Infantry. This was the first of many opportunities I had to work closely with your son and his crew.

    Before we departed to Iraq, I wanted as much training time with the Bradleys as possible. We worked many arduous hours in the Bradley simulators on post. This is where my mounted crews, consisting of 11 soldiers and me, became close. We talked about our families and our experiences; DJ spoke of all of you often. As the days turned into months, we continued to train for our departure.

    After our arrival in Iraq, our work schedule and threat level became very intense with little sleep and no time off to speak of; we went from mission to mission. These types of missions were long and very trying. This was a very difficult time for leaders and soldiers alike. The soldiers were tired, things would change on a moment's notice, and to keep them motivated was a challenge, to say the least. In 18 years, it has not been an uncommon sight for me. To hear soldiers complain and get upset is an almost regular occurrence. It is even said if an infantry soldier isn't complaining, he isn't happy; that is except for your son. Of all the soldiers in my platoon, I never heard your son complain. With the eating of MRE's for two straight months, and drinking hot water every day, DJ never made a derogatory word or comment.

    The good soldiers always tend to stand out above the rest. In the time I have had in the Army, I have had very few soldiers that have really grabbed my attention; your son was one of those soldiers. The way DJ would master tasks quickly and without much guidance made it a treat to work with him. No matter what the situation or the task asked of him, he would accomplish it and exceed the standard each and every time without hesitation or reservation. He was the type of soldier that was a dream for a leader – no complaints, no gripes, and he worked hard with no supervision needed (a young leader himself!!)

    It takes a different type of person to volunteer to be an Infantryman; it is a tough and thankless job. On one particular occasion during a combat patrol, a situation arose where DJ's quick thinking, reaction, and driving skill saved lives and kept the soldiers in the rear of his Bradley and his crew safe. This was his action and his alone, a true HERO in all our eyes. DJ's comment to this was he was just doing his job and nothing more. This was the type of team player he was. The men of 2nd Platoon and Charlie

Company, 1-22 Infantry, will never forget the impact DJ made on our lives. With this letter, you are receiving the awards that were presented at your

son's memorial service in Tikrit, Iraq. **1.**The Purple Heart is awarded to the members of the armed forces of the U.S. who are wounded by an instrument of war in the hands of the enemy and posthumously to the next of kin in the name of those who are killed in action or die of wounds received in action. It is specifically a combat decoration.

2. The Bronze Star is awarded to any person who, while serving in any capacity in, or with, the Army of the United States after December, 1941, distinguished himself or herself by heroic or meritorious achievement or service, not involving participation in aerial flight, in connection with military operations against an armed enemy; or while engaged in military operations involving conflict with an opposing armed force in which the United States is not a belligerent party. The Combat Infantryman's Badge (CIB) was established by the War Department on 27 October, 1943. Lieutenant General Lesley J. McNair, then the Army Ground Forces Commanding General, was instrumental in its creation. He originally recommended that it be called the "fighter badge." Then Secretary of War Henry Stinson said, *"It is high time we recognize in a personal way the skill and heroism of the American Infantry."* It is presently awarded to Infantrymen who serve in the line of enemy fire.

If there is anything I can do, or if you feel there are any questions that I could answer, please feel free to contact me at any time. I want to say again how very sorry we all are for the loss of your son. He was a true friend, brother, and outstanding soldier.   Sincerely,

TRIBUTE: CPL WILLIAM VELEZ TO HONOR
SPC DONALD L. "DJ"WHEELER, JR., COMPANY C
OCTOBER 2003 TIKRIT, IRAQ AND JUNE 2004 FORT HOOD,TEXAS

**CPL Velez of C Company, 1-22 Infantry,
bids farewell to fellow soldiers.
Photo taken in October 2003 by EPA's Stefan Zaklin.**
(vets4victory.com)

I lost one of my best friends (and this is the second time I have to speak in his behalf) and it breaks my heart every time. But it something I have to do because knowing DJ was a privilege that I want to share with as many people as I can. As a soldier DJ was competent, a hard worker, and fast learner. He started as a driver and I thought he was going to have a hard time driving because he was too tall, but he made it work. One of the best drivers I've ever seen.

His dedication and motivation got him promoted to Specialist in nineteen months. With good knowledge of the Bradley and always paying attention to details, he was ready to be a gunner and I was very happy that my driver had become my wingman. He was always looking to improve himself as a soldier by enrolling in the E Army U *(DJ was looking into college classes)* and even studying for the promotion board when he was a Private First Class *(striving to be all that he could be while in the Army)* and he was looking into transitioning to the Warrant Officer field in order to become an Apache helicopter pilot. He was a true soldier who came into this Army out of true patriotism.

As a friend, DJ was the best. Always ready to help everybody else even if it meant to stay awake late or wake up early. He loved playing video games and board games. He was also looking forward to next summer. He wanted to get married, buy a motorcycle and a truck, get a college degree. He was full of hopes and dreams. And he was focused into making those dreams into a reality.

I'll always remember DJ as a great soldier and a best friend. I'll also remember how high is the price of our freedom. DJ will be always in my heart and I'll pray for him and his family. It was an honor to serve with Specialist Wheeler. DJ will never be forgotten.

1ST BATTALION 22ND INFANTRY

1-22 soldiers grieve at a Memorial Service held in Tikrit on October 16, for SPC Donald Laverne Wheeler, Jr., killed by a rocket-propelled grenade on October 13, and for SPC James E. Powell, killed by an anti-tank mine on October 12. The two soldiers' helmets were placed together with their name tags over their rifle butts, next to their boots on a small podium adorned with the U.S. Flag and the regimental banner. Medals, including the Bronze Star and the Purple Heart, were awarded posthumously to Wheeler and Powell, and placed next to their rifles. *By Roberto Schmidt/AFP/Getty*

AS I REFLECT BACK ON THE LAST COUPLE OF YEARS

I

FIND

IT IS

FULL

OF

EXAMPLES

OF

GOD'S
MIGHTY HAND

EVER PRESENT,
GENTLY
LEADING US
TO THAT
FATEFUL DAY,

OCTOBER 13,2003,

and

THROUGHOUT
THE TIME SINCE.

"YOUR STRONG RIGHT HAND HAS UPHELD ME, LORD"
(Ps. 18:35).
AMEN! ALLELUIA!

89

Headquarters
Combined Joint Task Force Seven
Baghdad, Iraq
Office of the Commanding General
Ricardo S. Sanchez
Lieutenant General, US Army
Commanding

Dear Mr. And Mrs. Wheeler,   30 October 2003
The members of Victory Corps join me in extending our deepest sympathy on the death of your son, Specialist Donald L. Wheeler, Charlie Company, 1st Battalion, 22d Infantry Regiment, 4th Infantry Division. It is our hope you will understand how saddened we are by your son's death. We share in your loss. In time, may you find personal reassurance in the thought that his service to our nation was outstanding, and that our gratitude is deep and lasting.
The soldiers of Victory Corps and I extend our heartfelt condolences in your time of grief.

OCTOBER 31, 2003 A Memorial Service was held at Fort Hood, Texas. Only four of us attended since a decision was made to fly, not drive.

SPC James Powell
SPC Donald Wheeler, Jr.
1-22 Infantry Battalion, 4th Infantry Division (M)
Fort Hood, Texas 76544

31 Oct 03   **1400 Hrs**

ORDER OF SERVICE
PRELUDE   RUTH FRY
WELCOME   CHAPLAIN(MAJ) SPENCER HARDAWAY
*INVOCATION   CHAPLAIN (MAJ) SPENCER HARDAWAY
THE READINGS
Old Testament: Psalm 46   CPL Dax Allcorn
God is our refuge and our strength, an ever-present help in distress. Thus we do not fear, though earth be shaken and mountains quake to the depths

*of the sea, though its waters rage and foam and mountains totter at its surging. Streams of the river gladden the city of God, the holy dwelling of the Most High. God is in its midst; it shall not be shaken; God will help it at break of day. Though nations rage and kingdoms totter, He utters His Voice and the earth melts. The Lord of hosts is with us; our stronghold is the God of Ja*cob. *Come and see the works of the Lord, Who has done fearsome deeds on earth;Who stops wars to the ends of the earth, breaks the bow, splinters the spear, and burns the shields with fire;* **"Be still and know that I am God! I am exalted among the nations, exalted on the earth."**
The Lord of hosts is with us; our stronghold is the God of Jacob.

New Testament: Matthew 11:25-30   *CPL Dax Allcorn*
   At that time Jesus said in reply, "I give praise to You, Father, Lord of Heaven and earth, for although You have hidden these things from the wise and the learned You have revealed them to the childlike. Yes, Father, such has been Your gracious Will. All things have been handed over to Me by My Father. No one knows the Son except The Father, and no one knows The Father except the Son and anyone to whom the Son wishes to reveal Him. Come to Me, all you who labor and are burdened, and I will give you rest. Take My yoke upon you and learn from Me, for I am meek and humble of heart; and you will find rest for yourselves. For My yoke is easy, and My burden light."

Commander's Tribute
4th Infantry Division Rear Det. Commander   COL. Daniel Shanahan
1st Brigade Rear Det Commander   MAJ David Nguyen
1-22 Infantry Rear Det. Commander   CPT Matthew Weber
      Soldier's Tribute
  Remembrance of SPC James Powell   SPC Timothy Moore
  Remembrance of SPC Donald Wheeler, Jr.   CPL William Velez
           (page 87)
Prayer   Chaplain (1LT) Randall Ridenour
Meditation   Chaplain (MAJ) Carlton Hall
Silent Tribute
Closing Hymn   Ruth Fry
*Benediction   Chaplain (LTC) Alberto Cordova
Postlude   Ruth Fry

Please remain in your seats until departure of the Official Party
(*Congregation, Please Stand if you are able)

SPC Donald L. Wheeler Jr.

SPC Donald L. Wheeler Jr., affectionately known to friends and family as DJ, was born in Concord, Michigan, on July 15, 1981. Following graduation from high school, he worked as a machine operator at Concord Manufacturing Company. Motivated by events of September 11th, he entered the Army at Fort Benning, Georgia, in November 2001. SPC Wheeler completed basic training in April, 2002, and was assigned to 2nd Platoon, Charlie Company, 1st Battalion, 22nd Infantry Regiment at Fort Hood, TX. He served as an M249 automatic rifleman, Bradley driver, and Bradley gunner. He participated in Charlie Company's deployment to Cuba from October to December 2002. His awards include the Army Good Conduct Medal, Army Service Ribbon, Overseas Service Ribbon, Purple Heart, Bronze Star Medal, Track Vehicle Driver's Badge and Combat Infantryman's Badge. SPC Donald L. Wheeler Jr., the fourth of 12 children, is survived by his parents, Don and Marycay Wheeler, and his siblings: Burt, Trevor, Andrea (Jake) Barrett, Phyllis, Thomas, Quentin, Paul, Bernadette, Spencer, Dominic, and Patrick.

SPC James E. Powell

SPC James E. Powell was born in Columbus, Ohio, on February 27, 1977. Following graduation from high school, he served four years as a gunner's mate in the Navy. His love of the military prompted him to re-enter the service. He entered the Army at Fort Benning, Georgia, in January 2001. SPC Powell completed basic training in May 2001, and was assigned to 1st Platoon, Bravo Company, 1st Battalion, 22nd Infantry Regiment at Fort Hood, TX. SPC Powell served as a rifleman and Bradley driver. He participated in Bravo Company's deployments to the national Training Center in February 2002, and to Cuba from April to June 2002. His awards include the Army Good Conduct Medal, Army Service Ribbon, Overseas Service Ribbon, Purple Heart, Bronze Star Medal, and Combat Infantryman's Badge. SPC James E. Powell is survived by his wife, Ruby, and their two year-old daughter, Lauren.

"THE SHEPHERD'S PSALM"

The Lord is my Shepherd: I shall not want.
He maketh me to lie down in green pastures:
He leadeth me beside the still waters.
He restoreth my soul: He leadeth me in the
paths of righteousness for His Name's sake.
Yea, though I walk through the valley of the
shadow of death, I will fear no evil:
for Thou art with me;
Thy rod and Thy staff they comfort me.

Thou preparest a table before me
in the presence of mine enemies:
Thou annointest my head with oil;
my cup runneth over.
Surely goodness and mercy shall follow me
all the days of my life:
and I will dwell in the House of the Lord forever.(Ps 23)

During this time we met a couple of DJ's buddies. 1SG Michael Evans met us at our hotel and shared that he was the one that zipped DJ into the body bag. So a "Michael" was actually the last one who saw DJ in Tikrit, Iraq – wow! Another reminder that Saint Michael never left his side. I had wondered about DJ's religious medal and his rosary. He said he remembered seeing brown beads around but, not being religious, he did not know their significance and thus did not pick them up. It did my heart good to hear that he saw part of the rosary that DJ patted in his pocket the day of his deployment that gave me the strength to say goodbye. In retrospect, as I began to put the pieces together of that infamous day I was made aware that DJ's body was moved several times. Therefore, I wonder if 1SG Evans was extending some much needed compassion to a grieving mom. Again illustrating the fact that being part of the military means being part of a big family and for that I lovingly say, *"Thank you, Michael."*

Following Evans' visit there were a couple of other soldiers who came to the hotel. Seeing these young men, my mother's heart took over. They had been through so much but yet their willingness to share their memories with the parents of their buddy reminded me that once you are part of the Military you are family. Though perfect strangers, we are forever united in our hearts. They were able to inform me that DJ's religious medal and cross that hung in his Bradley had been collected by CPL William Velez. He knew their significance to DJ and to me so his intent was to place them directly in my hands.

Do you see what I mean when I say *"family"*? In the midst of their own loss they were able to think of me and how to help me. Such self-less love. May God bless them always.

CHAPTER SEVEN: WHEN DARKNESS FALLS FOLLOW THE STAR

NOVEMBER 2003

On November 8, 2003, I was inducted into a club. I am not a fan of "clubs" but this one was offered to me because of DJ's sacrifice so how could I refuse. The whole family was invited to a dinner and then after a couple of speeches I was called forward and given a banner with red trim with a gold star in the middle of a white rectangle. Alone with the banner I received a new title, too. I am now and forever more a "Gold Star Mom". A star given to me from DJ and I can see him smiling as he says, *"Shine on the world like a bright star, Mom, you offer it the Word of Life."*

IMPORTANT NOTE: In 2006 I attended a religious retreat and after receiving our first assignment we formed into groups of eight. A woman approached my group and asked, "Who here knows a 'DJ'?" I waited a moment and then spoke up. Now looking at me, "I have a message for you from Blessed Mary." My eyebrows raised as she continued. "She wants you to know that DJ is with you."

This woman, motivated by the still, small Voice, confirmed what I already knew. Ever since October 13, 2003, by a special Grace from God, I had been aware of a "light." My own "miracle of the sun." That's why DJ's nickname is still true – *"SUNSHINE"*!

I pray by receiving this title, DJ, you will help me to begin to shine as well as you do. **All for God's Glory!**

I had stayed away from listening to the news for a couple of weeks. Then, still with no desire, I found myself sitting in the same chair that I had heard, *"A **Gunner** in Tikrit has died"*, reached for the remote and turned on the TV "needing" to listen to the news. The very first face I saw was LTC Steve Russell, in battle gear, concluding an interview from Tikrit with these words,

"...I'm here to remind them the Tiger has teeth."

The best way I can attempt to explain what affect those words had on me is that I felt like I had been in a wrestling match and I had been pinned so forcefully to the ground that the wind was knocked out of me. LTC Russell resuscitated me. I was not only hearing the Commander of the Army but a Daddy whose heart was broken due to seeing too many of his children having been injured or killed and it had to stop. His words came from that love and that is why I felt a connection. I knew DJ had not left the battle for a moment and it was time for me to join him. So I put on my spiritual Armor with the intent to strengthen LTC Russell and DJ's buddies. Saddam Hussein's days were numbered! I had no doubt.

DECEMBER 5

It was a cold day with intermittent snow showers and I was preparing for a son's 17th birthday. With dinner cooking and cake baked, I was wrapping the final presents when the phone rang. It sucked the breath out of me. It was Mayflower Moving Company making sure someone was home to receive a shipment from Fort Hood, Texas. It was a good thing that I was well-organized because I was stunned. With the kids at school I would be the only one to receive all that was left of DJ's life at Fort Hood. How did I prepare for this? I sat in the living room across from the altar in stillness and waited. Within an hour the truck was there.

It was snowing now but it was not a concern. I went out the front door, down the steps, and stood on the sidewalk so as to stay out of the driver's way as he maneuvered the big truck so the side doors could face the sidewalk.

Mayflower, is an interesting name – a word that conjures up feelings of hope. Hope for the pilgrims to live in Freedom. What bravery those people had to leave all they knew to face the unknown. That is the caliber of people that helped form our nation, the root that helped

America to grow and flourish. I mused how appropriate it was for DJ's belongs to be entrusted to this company. His spirit,his root, his foundation reflects that of the pilgrims – willing to face the unknown for the sake of Freedom. But not for himself but for people on the other side of the world – the Iraqi's.

IMPORTANT NOTE: In the year 2006 I heard that Americans of Iraqi descent from Detroit were to visit Saint Joseph Church in Jackson to have a Mass to pray for their country. I knew I had to attend. *My son flew to the other side of the world to fight for their country's freedom, the least I could do was drive four miles to pray with them for their country and for their families still in Iraq.* Upon their arrival my ears were filled with a foreign language. I became very emotional. I now had the "sounds" that DJ would have heard while deployed. *God is good!*

I could not go inside. I just opened the front doors and directed the men to the living room. I already had my camera so I headed back outside with the intent to document this last piece of DJ's life so as to share it with the kids. I was speechless and so were the men. They worked methodically and professionally as they opened a plywood box which contained wooden pieces that would form a desk. Cardboard box after cardboard box were carried into the house. Standing with the snow falling on my Fort Hood sweatshirt, I soaked in not only the snowflakes but tried to soak in this scene while tears ran down my face.

One of the three men approached me with a clipboard and said, *"That's it, ma'am. Please sign here."* as he pointed at the paper. The other men closed the front door and headed to the truck. As I took the clipboard I nodded and signed the paper. I put my hand out to shake his and thanked him and they prepared to leave. I headed to the house slowly. Once they closed all the doors of the truck, they climbed in and proceeded down the driveway as my nostrils were filled with the exhaust. Opening the front door, a new smell overwhelmed me – wet cardboard. I stepped into the foyer and stared. The living room looked more like a warehouse now. I walked into the doorway and sat on the floor and stared as I read "WHEELER" on box after box. I looked at DJ's picture standing behind the couch that we used at his sister's wedding. I could almost hear him say to me, **"Be strong, Mom. It'll all work out in the end."** which left me feeling at peace.

Later, when everyone was home, we had a different kind of party. We took turns opening box after box, slowly and reverently. Things that were last touched by DJ and were never going to be again. A box that I opened had a card laying on top. It was a Christmas card that I sent him in 2002. And now, twenty days from Christmas, 2003, I heard DJ in my heart saying, **"Merry Christmas, Mom."**

SUNDAY, DECEMBER 13, 2003

I had gotten up early this morning and was walking on my ellipse when I began to flipping through the channels on the television when I came across a news broadcast with a special report:

BREAKING NEWS FROM IRAQ:
"Ladies and gentlemen, we got him."

I jumped off the ellipse and started hootin' and hollerin.' Running downstairs, I banged on every bedroom door. I wanted everyone up as I ran to turn on the TV in the living room, clapping and yelling,

"They found Saddam! They got him!"

Kids began to join me in celebrating, but much more subdued. I saw the barn lights were on so I knew a son was about to leave to go hunting. I ran outside to tell him and give him a hug. A great morning in American history and DJ and his buddies were front and center!

OPERATION IRAQI FREEDOM
Battalion Commander, LTC Steven D. Russell
1st Battalion, 22nd Infantry, Tikrit, Iraq
Reflections of December 13, 2003

http://1- 22infantry.org/current/updatedec25.htm

The morning of the 13th I received a phone call from my commander. I listened as COL Hickey explained the snowball of information now gathering. He told me to alert my soldiers for any contingency and to have a force ready at a moment's notice. He planned to use us and the brigade reconnaissance troop, which he would bring down from the western desert. We were going after the alligator. *(They had drained many swamps to find insurgents and had much success, even though there were alligators, too. But the "alligator" they were in pursuit of was Saddam Hussein)*

We had been through the drill many times before. Des Bailey and I had worked together on many a raid in the farmlands east, across the Tigris. Each time an excitement builds because each time could be the catch. Not two days before I had told the press that there was an intensity and excitement about Saddam comparable to our operations in July and August during the well-publicized hunt for him. Sensing my honesty about the matter, though no facts were conveyed, several decided to hang around Tikrit despite the urging of their editors. They were not sorry they did.

COL Hickey told me that we could expect something in west Tikrit —that's about what he knew as to the locale. As soon as he had better information, we would act swiftly. By late afternoon the information came. But the location had changed from west Tikrit to east Tikrit and across the Tigris River. We kept a ready force on our side and opposite Ad Dawr. COL Hickey proceeded to assemble the forces on the east side for the operation. Special operations forces and brigade elements that included LTC Reggie Allen's 1-10 Cavalry, LTC Dom Pompelia's 4-42 Field Artillery with attached engineers (Dom was still on leave and so his exec, MAJ Steve Pitt, would command the artillery soldiers), and CPT Des Bailey's G Troop, 10th Cavalry readied for the operation, commencing at 2000 hours.

Our brigade elements provided the cordon *(a cordon is a line of people to surround the area, to close, or guard it)* while the special

98

operations folks hit two farmhouses. In the courtyard of one was the now famous hole from which a haggard Saddam Hussein was pulled. The special ops soldiers pulled him away and then whisked him off to safety. COL Hickey ordered the site to be secured for future exploitation. He called MG Ray Odierno and gave him the good news. While I suspected as much because of the orders we were receiving on the radio, it was not until about 2230 that COL Hickey phoned and broke the good news. "Sid Caeser!" he said (in the summer time frame, the higher command published 'what if' pictures of Saddam if he tried to change his appearance. COL Hickey often joked that one of them looked like Sid Caesar).

 "Oh my God!" I said as I thanked God silently while the boss explained what happened.

 "Not a word," he said. *"The announcement must be official and it will take some time."*

 "Roger, sir. I understand the importance of it."

 Contained, self-composed, but about to bust at the seams as I hung up the phone, I kept silent to the men about the news that would change the world. I felt proud and thankful to have been a part of it from the beginning. I could not help but think back to an email that I received from my wife in late October. She said that a man named Dick Dwinnell called her and encouraged her to send me a message. In it, he said that he knew **I was a praying man** and as a leader, one of my missions was to find Hussein. He said that if my staff and **I prayed for God to help us find Saddam, He would help us.** That next Sunday we did just that. I asked the brigade chaplain, MAJ (CH) Oscar Arauco to lead us. For the next several weeks he continued to lead us until our battalion chaplain, CPT (CH) Tran returned to us from an illness. And now here I was taking it all in on the evening of the **13th of December. *"Psalm 33:16-22"*.**

**TWO MONTHS AFTER MY SON,
SPC DONALD L. WHEELER, JR.'S
BIRTH INTO ETERNAL LIFE WHERE HE WAS IN A
BETTER POSITION TO GOD'S EAR AND WE ALL
REMEMBER THE IMPORTANCE THE NUMBER 13 IS TO
OUR OUR LADY OF FATIMA,
THE BLESSED VIRGIN MARY, THE MOTHER OF GOD.
THROUGH HER IMMACULATE HEART
THERE WILL BE PEACE ON EARTH.**

Thanks for listening, dear Lord, to the pleading of a soldier who gave his all for his country and his buddies.
       Amen! Alleluia! All Glory and Honor to God!

"FOR NOT BY THEIR OWN SWORD DID THEY WIN THE LAND;
NOR DID THEIR OWN ARM GIVE THEM VICTORY;
BUT THY RIGHT HAND, AND THY ARM,
AND THE LIGHT OF THY COUNTENANCE;
FOR THOU DIDST DELIGHT IN THEM. "(Ps 44:3)

IMPORTANT NOTE: I was told by the mother in California that DJ's buddies arrived home on the 12th of March making the first full day of being home from Iraq the <u>13th</u> of March, 2004.

DECEMBER 2003

For the Christmas card I added a collage of pictures of DJ growth from a toddler into a man and one of his sun pictures he took in Cuba. A keepsake for my family and friends in remembrance of DJ. Things might not work out like we plan but we must keep our eyes on The Son in loving trust and hope uniting everything to The Cross of Jesus Christ.

JANUARY 2004 DJ AND OUR LADY OF ALL NATIONS

"Father, He who knew no sin was made sin for us, to save us and restore us to Your friendship. Look at our contrite heart and afflicted spirit and heal our troubled conscience, so that in the joy and strength of the Holy Spirit we may proclaim Your Praise and Glory before ALL NATIONS"
(Div Off Vol IV pg 755).

A niece was contemplating being a religious which made her cross paths with a couple of sisters from Europe. In their conversations she took the opportunity to talk about her cousin that gave "the ultimate gift for his country" along with his words from his letters. They were so moved by DJ's story they requested to meet *the mom*. Meeting religious sisters, I thought, could only help our family. Their prayers had to be powerful since God was their Bridegroom – how could He say no to any of their requests. So January 22, 2004, my youngest daughter and I went to spend a couple of days in prayer with them and to share more of DJ's words, pictures, and stories. It was the story about the Flag that touched their hearts. DJ and his buddies being commended because of the reverence and respect they showed it and then my "inspired" words to DJ, that someday the Flag would honor him that caused Sr. Brigitta to make this observation,

"As Our Lady of All Nations, Blessed Mary, wears a Sash tied around Her waist representing the Loincloth which Jesus wore at His Crucifixion. Your love for the Flag because it was the last thing you have that "touched" DJ reminds me of Blessed Mary's love for that Cloth, the last thing that touched Her Son. The love of Mothers' for their Sons' sacrifice motivates this reverence."

I thanked her for her kindness for finding any similarity between Blessed Mary and myself. Since I had never heard of Our Lady of All Nations I asked for more information. She explained the purpose of these apparitions our Heavenly Mother is asking us, Her children, to petition Jesus and the Holy Spirit to help ALL NATIONS through this prayer:

Lord Jesus Christ, Son of the Father send now Your Spirit over the earth. Let the Holy Spirit live in the hearts of all nations, that they may be preserved from degeneration, disaster and war. May the Lady of All Nations,who once was Mary,be our Advocate. Amen.

Her Motherly concern touched my heart. I wanted to help Her Voice to be heard. In union with DJ, whose love for our nation propelled him to fight, it is only fitting to do whatever I can.

"Evil thrives when good men do nothing."
(Edmund Burke)

When I got home I did more research on Our Lady of All Nations: *"The picture shows some sheep who represent the people of the world who will not find rest or achieve contentedness until they fix their eyes on the Cross, the center of this world... The palms of Her hands rays of light stream-out, three from each hand, and diffuse themselves upon the sheep... These three rays are Grace, Redemption and Peace"(May 31, 1951). And, later on, She reminds us," **to come to the foot of the Cross and draw strength from The Sacrifice"** (February 17, 1952) – the same strength Our Mother received when She was at the foot of the Cross of Her Son, Our Lord Jesus Christ!*

As the carpet of snow melts into the ground, so will the Fruit [Peace] that the Holy Spirit brings into the hearts of all nations who <u>say this prayer every day</u>!... You cannot estimate the value this prayer will have... It has been given for the benefit of all nations... for the conversion of the world... Do your work and see to it that it is made known everywhere... The Son demands obedience!... The Blessed Trinity will reign over the world again!" (The 1951 messages of The Lady of All Nations.)

On February 3, 2004, Blessed Mary came to me in a dream resembling Our Lady of Medugorje. *(DJ was born in 1981, the year when Blessed Mary began appearing in Medugorje, June 24th the Feast Day of Saint John the Baptist who preached, "Repent.")* Without moving Her Mouth I heard,

"NO ONE'S LISTENING."

I felt Her sadness and woke crying and perplexed. *"What am I supposed to do?"* An opportunity arose when a monument was dedicated to DJ and all Veterans of War on Memorial Day, 2004. With knees knocking and voice quivering I spoke, among other things, Blessed Mary's Message as Our Lady of All Nations and had my children pass out Our Lady of All Nations holy cards. Over the years when it is DJ's Anniversary I have made Memorial cards putting DJ on one side and Our Lady of All Nations on the other. I pray it will get people to *listen.*

Within the prayer to Our Lady of All Nations there is a phrase, *"...Lady Who once was Mary..."* Some people thought it was wrong but I understand Blessed Mary's desire. As much as I love my children, my heart has been open to the plight of *all* children. I want not only to be known as a Mother to 13 but to many: *military, unborn, abused, alcoholics, lonely, religious, cancer patients, etc.* I feel the Lord has impregnated me with the concerns and pains of many children. My desire is to be able to be in a position that will amplify my voice as I say the prayers Blessed Mary and Saint Michael have taught us so as to reach God's Ear.

"...so shall My Word he that goes forth from My mouth; It shall not return to Me empty but It shall accomplish that which I purpose, and prosper in the thing for which I sent It" (Is 55 :11).

So say the prayer no matter who you are because:

The *"longer [Catholics] wait [to fulfill the Lady's requests], the more the Faith will decline; the greater the number of years, the greater the apostasy"* (August 15, 1951). *To you all [Catholics], however, falls the task of introducing 'The Lady of All Nations' to the whole world"* (February 17, 1952)

(All quotes: ww.ourladyofallnations.org)

102

FEBRUARY 2004 DJ'S HEADSTONE

The task at hand was the design of DJ's headstone. We had decided to have Saint Michael etched on the left *(as you look at it)*, Our Lady of All Nations carved 3-D in the middle and an etching of The Bible and rosary on the right. So while the kids were in school I went to the monument dealer. All was going along just fine until it came to the image of Saint Michael. The salesperson could only find pictures of Saint Michael standing with sword at his side. That was not the Michael I had been envisioning helping DJ all these years. I asked if I could bring a holy card showing her how I envisioned the Archangel and she agreed.

When I got home to an empty house I went directly into the living room and plopped down on the couch across from the altar. I felt disgusted and emotionally worn out. As I looked up I gestured in the direction of the altar where DJ's statue from Confirmation was and said out loud,

"Everyone knows that Saint Michael looks like that."

As I said those words it was like a veil dropped from my eyes and I saw it for the first time, now nine years later. The curly, blond-haired Angel with eyes raised to Heaven as he stands on top of rocks, which I interpreted to mean a mountaintop, holding his sword and shield over his head praising God for a Victory. When the kids got home I asked,

"How come no one ever questioned me about the statue I gave DJ? It doesn't look like any image we have ever seen of Saint Michael."
They just shrugged their shoulders. But as I looked at it from where we were nine years later, I can truly say it is DJ's Saint Michael. Victorious! So after further discussion, I asked,

"Which image do we want on DJ's headstone,
the fighting Saint Michael or DJ's Victorious Saint Michael?"
The vote was unanimous, *"DJ's Saint Michael!"*

If there was ever any doubt in anyone's mind about DJ's vocation as an American Soldier it can be laid to rest. God's Plan for his life had been fulfilled.

CHAPTER EIGHT: REMEMBERING

The following are excerpts from letters we received.

"DJ's willingness to serve his country will continue to strengthen soldier's lives for many years to come."
Jack L. Tilley, 12th Sergeant Major of the Army

"Specialist Wheeler was a devoted soldier committed to defending our country, and he made the ultimate sacrifice while preserving freedom. Your son gave his very best for America. We are proud of him."
Donald Rumsfeld, Secretary of Defense

"His service and sacrifice to this nation was for a just cause, our people. Donald was a true patriot, an integral part of his platoon, and left an everlasting impression on everyone he ever associated with. He will never be replaced. I'm extremely proud to have known him. Donald was the epitome of a soldier and patriot. A True American Hero... He was truly a role model for all U.S. citizens through his love and dedication to his country."
Raymond T. Odierno, Major General, U.S. Army, Commanding, 4th Infantry Division

"I am deeply saddened by the loss of your son, Specialist Donald L. Wheeler, Jr., USA. DJ's noble service in Operation Iraqi Freedom has helped to preserve the security of our homeland and the freedoms America holds dear. Our Nation will not forget DJ's sacrifice and unselfish dedication in our efforts to make the world more peaceful and free. We will forever honor his memory. Laura and I send our heartfelt sympathy. We hope you will be comforted by your faith and the love and support of your family and friends. May God bless you."
George W. Bush, President of the United States of America

I responded to the President's letter. He has the power to send many thousands of Americans into battle. I felt he needed to implement the winning formula presented by Our Lady of Fatima and in the end save thousands, if not millions, of lives. I was not expecting a reply but I prayed that the intent of my actions, which were to express love for my son, the military, and our Nation, would be understood. *America needs to wake up.* The original letter was much longer because I had to humanize DJ from "just another soldier that died for his country." Since all those facts have been explained in this book I will go to the main point.

Dear Mr. President and Mrs. Laura Bush,   November 10, 2003
Thank you for your kind expression of sadness about our son, Specialist Donald Laverne Wheeler, Jr.'s ultimate sacrifice in the streets of Tikrit, Iraq. I know you have had to write too many of these letters lately... DJ, our nickname for our son, was very eager to help our country... My son learned something over there in Iraq and it is his message that God is propelling me to speak for him once again since his voice is silenced forever. A message that all America needs to hear. The date of DJ's birth into Eternal Life, October 13th, was the last appearance of Our Heavenly Mother, Blessed Mary in Fatima, Portugal. The core of the message from Blessed Mary, if you are not familiar, is explained by an Archbishop:

'If we do not reject the path of sin: hatred, revenge, injustice, violations of the rights of the human person, immorality, and violence, etc.; let us remember it is not God who is punishing us it is the people preparing their own punishment. In God's kindness He is warning us and calling us to the "right path", while allowing our freedom to choose. Hence people are responsible. Blessed Mary reminds us that man's future is in God, and that we are active and responsible partners in creating that future.'

(Tarcisio Bertone,SDB, Archbishop Emeritus of Vercelli, Secretary of the Congregation for the Doctrine of the Faith.)

...The walls of Jericho came crashing down because Joshua and his people followed God's directions. Blessed Mary has the directions and we must follow them. It may seem impossible for man but nothing is impossible for God....Quote from one of DJ's letters is:

"Someone is watching over us over here. I can feel Him."

God wants to help us. But He needs us to do our part. Listen to Blessed Mary's Words. Draw our weapons which are our arms opened to God and our voices raised in humble prayer and trust Him. Good will triumphant over evil – of that we can be confident. Then praise and give all the glory to God. If we do, then DJ's words expressing his total confidence and Trust in God, will come true,

"It'll all work out in the end."

MARCH 2004

DJ was nominated as one of their **"Everyday Heroes"** by the Red Cross of Michigan for the year 2003. The night included a dinner and a video filmed at the local television station presenting the stories of all the nominees. To present his story as an American Soldier meant going through all of DJ's Army things. Rereading letters and cards received in the last four months, looking through picture after picture to make a collage depicting DJ's life. It felt like a project I would help the kids with for school and I found myself looking for DJ to walk into the living room at any minute to say,

105

"Hey, Mom, need help?"

Truly a labor of love that tore at my heart but it needed to be done and since no one else volunteered it fell on me. Then it became clear to me that if they wanted to remember him they first needed to know him. So I put together a short story about DJ before and after being an American Soldier as a keepsake for all who would attend the dinner. After writing it, I took it to the college where I had been taking classes working toward a teaching degree, seeking advice. Because of their compassionate hearts they offered to print and assemble the booklet for me. Praise God!

BAKER COLLEGE OF JACKSON, THANK YOU!

To know DJ meant knowing his brothers and sisters so the night before the filming, a month or so before the dinner, I called all the kids into the living room. I wanted them to be front and center in this video so I had chosen several letters to be read or they could share their own thoughts. But before proceeding with reading the choices, I began speaking about the *Gift* of DJ's death. *These words were not mine and the words that follow were not something I had intended to speak – evidence of the still, small Voice.* I said it is like the parable about the **"rich man and Lazarus"**. The rich man's only concern was for his own livelihood and neglected the needs of those around him - like the poor man, Lazarus, whom he saw daily. When he died he looked up from the flames of hell and saw Lazarus, who had also died, sitting at the side of Abraham. The rich man now finding himself in need cries out, *(I paraphrased that night but now I am quoting),*

"Father Abraham, have mercy upon me, and send Lazarus to dip the end of his finger in water and cool my tongue; for I am in anguish in this flame." Abraham replied, *"Son, remember that you in your lifetime received your good things; and Lazarus in like manner evil things; but now he is comforted here and you are in anguish...besides between us and you a great chasm has been fixed..." "Then I beg you, Father, to send him to my father's house, for I have five brothers, so that he may warn them, lest they also come into this place of torment."* Abraham replied, *"They have Moses and the prophets; let them hear them." "No, Father Abraham; but if someone goes to them from the dead, they will repent."* He said to him, *"If they do not hear Moses and the prophets, neither will they be convinced if someone should rise from the dead"* (Luke 16:24-31).

DJ's death was our opportunity to make sure we kept our priorities in place. If DJ could come back and speak to us what would he say?

I am remembering, even as I share this with you, how bewildered I was trying to understand what that parable had to do with DJ. He was not someone who was only concerned about making money and ignored the needs of others. So I researched this topic and found five points that Monsignor Pope of Washington, D.C., gave on March 5, 2010 on Learning the Lessons of Lazarus and the Rich Man and share some of his words.

1.) **Neglect of the poor is a damnable sin.** His sin is a sin of neglect and omission. He seems undisturbed and remote from Lazarus' suffering... this insensitivity lands him in hell... Jesus says,
> *"Depart from Me, you who are cursed, into the eternal fire prepared for the devil and his angels"*(Matt 25:41).

How best to care for the poor is a matter of some dispute, but that we MUST care for them in some explicit way is not in dispute. Hence we find the rich man who sinfully neglected Lazarus now in hell. Here is a call to sobriety about the reality of judgment..."

2.) **Though in torment the rich man does not change.** He does not ask Abraham to send Lazarus to him so that he may apologize for his sinful neglect and seek his forgiveness. Rather he merely wants Lazarus to serve him. The rich man, though in torment is unrepentant. He doesn't like where he is but he remains unreconciled with Lazarus and seems to have no idea that he should even seek to be reconciled. He is hardened in his sin. While Lazarus lived he never saw his dignity. He is still blind to that dignity. Over time sin hardens our heart. The more we remain in sin the harder our hearts become and the less likely it is that we will ever change. Why is hell eternal? Look at the rich man. He will not change. He cannot change. His decision, his character and demeanor are forever fixed. There is an old litany that goes like this: *"Sow a thought, reap a deed; sow a deed, reap a habit; sow a habit, reap a character; sow a character, reap a destiny."* ...The Fathers of the Church spoke of this Mystery like clay on a potter's wheel. As long as the clay is moist and on the wheel the potter can shape and reshape it. But there comes a time when the clay is placed in the kiln and when it is fired its shape is forever fixed. It is this way for us when we come before God who judges us by fire (*cf* 1 Cor 3:12-15). Fire will forever fix who we are in terms of character and this judgment through fire (our crosses) will either purify us or bring us condemnation. The fixed quality

107

of the human person is illustrated in the rich man's attitude.

3.) Rich man does not ask to come to Heaven but wants Lazarus to come to hell. The saddest thing about people in hell is that they would not be happy in Heaven anyway. After all, Heaven is about being with God, it is about justice, love of the poor, chastity, the heavenly liturgy, the celebration of the truth, the praise of God, and God (rather than me) being at the center...

4.) The great reversal. We spend a lot of time trying to be on top in this world. We want comfort, wealth, position, power, and so forth. But the Lord warns that we ought to beware of the great reversal that is coming. Lazarus who was poor is now rich. We so want to be rich and comfortable in this world and we run from any suffering or setback. But the Lord warns of riches:

"How hard it is for the rich to enter the kingdom of God!"(Mk 10:23). Yet still we want to be rich. He also says,

"Anyone who does not carry his cross and follow Me cannot be My disciple"(Lk 14:27).

Yet still we run from the cross and suffering. Better to be found among the humble and poor.

5.) To refuse the Truth of revelations is a damnable sin. The rich man does not repent to God, neither does he seek to be reconciled with Lazarus. But he does have some concerns for his brothers, for his family. We need not assume that the souls in hell have no affections whatsoever. It simply remains true that their affections are not for God and what God esteems. And so the rich man, still seeing Lazarus only as an errand boy for his own needs, asks Abraham to dispatch Lazarus to his family with warning. Abraham says it clearly, there are many sinners who are hardened in their sin and no matter what the Scriptures say or what the Church solemnly teaches, they will never be convinced. This is so very true today as many remain hardened in their sins. No amount of Scripture or Church teaching will convince them that they are wrong. This is what happens to us if we remain in unrepentant sin. Our hearts are hardened, our minds are closed and our necks are stiffened. In the end, this story teaches that such hardness is damnable.

As I share Monsignor Pope's words I am once again humbled to realize how loving God is to allow the Gift of DJ's death to continue to speak, to teach and to direct.

After "my homily" I moved on to reading the letters and official declarations from the city and from the state. Everyone stepped forward and picked what they felt most comfortable reading. The next night we went to the filming all dressed in shirts and/or pants of DJ's army attire so his presence was deeply felt. I was very proud of how well the kids handled themselves in front of the camera since we are not "spotlight" type of people but we did it for DJ.

MARCH 25, 2004 RED CROSS DINNER:
EVERYDAY HEROES

The night of the dinner when the whole family was called forward I spoke these words that I had prepared:

Thank you for recognizing DJ as a hero. SPC Donald L. Wheeler, Jr. was a man committed to his vocation in life. Once committed, his integrity, character, and courage could be seen. All were based on his faith and love for God.

On October 13th, DJ's birth into Eternal Life, I really believe more men could have died. From the letter Capt. Boyd wrote, they knew two Iraqi's fired RPG's (rocket propelled grenades). There, in those last seconds, I really believe God performed DJ's first miracle – in those last crucial seconds, I believe DJ prayed, *"Take me, Lord! Don't harm my buddies!"* and God answered his prayer. **All** of his buddies were fine, even though they were only a few feet from the blast! And the Bradley was still drivable.

Then God, on that very same day, when our family was told, reminded us to continue to TRUST HIM. Then MORE miracles began to happen. DJ's handsome face and contagious smile may not be seen on earth anymore but he lives!

I can find him in the parents who brought their four children to the funeral home so they would never forget what it means to be an American and honor "a true American Hero"; a middle-aged woman, who approached me at school to tell me she had decided to become a Catholic; a teenager whose faith was strengthen and a religious teacher whose teenage students were very cynical until they heard about DJ. I embrace and love them all for uniting with us in our grief. Their hearts were opened because of DJ' sacrifice and an open heart allows God's Love to flow.

Are you questioning how did DJ achieve **peace?** His own words hold the answer and are a constant source of strength.

"I pray the rosary every day. It's the only way to stay sane out here."
DJ found his strength in his love for God and in return God made Himself known to DJ in a very personal way.

"Someone is watching over us over here. I can feel HIM."
God wants this relations with all His people, for all nations. We need to look

to God and PEACE can be found. DJ, himself, testifies to this TRUTH.

With the small booklet we put together, we hope his story is clearer to you. I pray your faith in God is strengthened because that is the gift DJ would want you to gain from his sacrifice.

In closing I want to share with you what happened just this week. We received a package that I sent to DJ back on September 30th. It arrived Saturday, March 20th a very significant day in our family because it is Bernadette's birthday. Bernadette says the package was, in a way, is her birthday present from DJ thanking her for the poem she wrote about him. *(page 73)* DJ always encouraged her writing talent. We know he is proud of her, as are we. Enclosed in the package was my letter. It is fitting to end this tribute to our son and my children's brother, DJ, SPC Donald L. Wheeler, Jr. with the words I wanted DJ to read because they are as true now as they were when I wrote them.

I LOVE YOU WITH EVERY BREATH I TAKE.
DJ, MY HERO!

As I had mentioned in my speech at the Red Cross Everyday Heroes dinner about a ***teenager whose faith was strengthen***. I was made aware of this because the mom sent me a copy of the paper that was written for a high school Honors English Class. These words encouraged me that at least one person understood – I trusted in God even though the evidence looked disastrous. I continue to proclaim that God is doing something truly powerful because I have retained a Joy and a Peace that no one can take from me. God is Good and I Trust Him.

"May the God of hope fill you with all joy and peace in believing, so that by the power of the Holy Spirit you may abound in hope"(Rom 15:13).

"The day was slowly winding down. I could see the light through the shades begin to dim as we lay there in the room bordered with colorful rainbows. My sister and I were tucked in under a pink canopy while my mom sat at the edge of our bed. The light from the closet, which was kept on through the night, danced across her face in the shadows.

'And thank You for being like scotch tape because you can't see it but you know it's there.'
This had wrapped up our conversation with God every night for at least a couple of years. I recited these words a number of times, not sure of their full meaning. But even at the tender age of seven, this strange thing inside of me, my Faith, was beginning to grow.

I remember asking my mom what those words meant...She told me that even though we hadn't see the Face of God, it was still possible to believe in Him. I recall trying with all my heart to believe that God was in my presence as I lay awake during a still night...I wanted so badly to see Him so that it wouldn't take so much work to believe.

Ten years later, I still have days when I would like God to be less like scotch tape, with its faded outline that is so hard to see. Even today there are countless times when I , like the rest of the world, would like God to be more like duct tape, with its darkened outline - its unmistakeable shape. It is difficult for us as human beings to accept that which we can not clearly see. Our minds are not always able to grasp God's mysterious ways. I think we all find it difficult to see the way that God chooses to work sometimes.

These days we have what I've heard called the "McDonald's Mentality."...Our needs are met within a few minutes. We live in an age where we have an abundance of information and knowledge at our fingertips. Thanks to the world wide web, we can pull up anything from World Wars to movie listings within seconds. Yet nowhere in a computer will you find the reasons for poverty and famine in third world countries or for terrorism in our homeland. There is no advance search for unanswered prayers. We rely on technology as the greatest form of communication though I have yet to receive God's email address in my Yahoo mailbox. He hasn't been found instant messaging my buddies...When we can't find the answers on our own, we either question our Faith or God's faithfulness. These are the times when we think,

'If only I had prayed longer. If only my Faith had been stronger' or
'If God was real He wouldn't have let this thing happen. If God cared about me He'd take me out of my set of circumstances.'

It is during these times it is easier to doubt than to trust, easier to get depressed than to press on. If we choose though to rise above and go beyond what is easy, our faith has the biggest impact on others and gives us the strength to stand.

I had the chance to see this kind of Faith through a neighbor and community member over the last few weeks. On October 13, 2003, a twenty-two year old soldier by the name of DJ Wheeler was killed in Iraq while defending our country. This young man was not only a hero but also a beloved son, an irreplaceable part of a special family. This person of Faith is not just a community member, she is a mom. A mom who held her son as a child, a mom who watched her baby grow into a highly respected American citizen and soldier, a mom who prayed for her son. That is why her testimony of Faith spoke so strongly to my heart. After finding out about her son's death, Mary Cay Wheeler could have reacted in a number of different ways. She could have been bitter and hateful, resenting God and others. And really, who would have blamed her? She could have pushed others away, yet she embraced those around her, allowing them to give her added strength and support. She could have placed blame on others and been mad at the world, yet she chose to uphold our country, giving others hope. She was able to see through the Eyes of God saying,

'evil was chosen but good will prevailed.'

It is through trials and temptations that we learn to trust. During the starless nights in our hearts we either give up on looking for glimpses of God or realize that our only hope for direction lies in relying on a higher Light. It is when we can't see the path that lies ahead that we reach out to allow His Divine Hand to guide our way.

I recently ran across these words which were written on a wall in a concentration camp. They represent a Faith that is unbreakable,

'I believe in the sun even when it is not shining.
I believe in love even when I feel it not.
I believe in God even when He is silent.'

How powerful these words are."

APRIL 2004

I received a phone call from the President of the Jackson Citizens for Life. She wanted to honor DJ for his selfless love for our Nation and for the freedom of the Iraqi people under the title, "Dignity of Life Award". DJ gave the ultimate gift, demonstrating his belief that all human beings are born in the image of God and therefore have the right to be treated with dignity from conception to natural death. Life is about choices and DJ set the example that is worth emulating. I applauded the idea.

"...and a little child will lead them"(Is 11:6).

JUNE 2004   MEMORIAL BALL, FORT HOOD, TEXAS

When we arrived at Fort Hood with all but two of my sons we stayed at a hotel on base. We were invited to dinner where several of DJ's buddies would be joining us. This is when William Velez placed items very dear to my heart in my hands. DJ's rosary was unrecoverable but his necklace, shaped in a Cross with the images of the Sacred Heart of Jesus, Our Lady of the Miraculous Medal, Saint Joseph and Saint Christopher with the Holy Spirit in the center, his *real* dog tags, and the Trinity Cross attached to a two-foot Iraqi rope that was knotted. William explained that DJ had gone through every rubbish pile in Iraq looking for something to hang the Cross next to him when he was the driver of the Bradley. I will never forget how Velez transferred them from his hands into mine saying,

"I knew these would be precious to you, as they were to DJ, so I couldn't trust the U. S. Post Office with the job. I had to do it."
He extended his hand, inviting me to place my hand in his, which I did. He then turned my hand so my palm was facing up. With his hand still cradling mine, he reached in different pockets to first place DJ's necklace then his dog-tags and finally laid the Trinity Crucifix on top. Our eyes met as he laid his hand on top of all these precious gifts. With tears streaming down my face I stood to hug him and thanked him over and over, and then sat back down to just look at them. I could feel DJ all around me. Finally, and I must admit reluctantly, I shared them with the kids. I wanted them back so I kept my eye on them as they made their way around the table. We ended our time together with a toast to the Soldier none of us will ever forget, DJ, SPC Wheeler.

The next day began with the Memorial Service held in the Main Base Chapel. I do not remember all the details of that service but what I received that morning is forever in my heart. First, CPL William Velez repeated his tribute he gave DJ when they were in Tikrit back in October, 2003. When the service was over, William handed me his speech *(page 87)*. A beautiful gift. Second, when I was making my way to leave, I stopped to hug or to shake hands with other families of the military. But one man made a point to come up and hugged me. Whatever words we exchanged is not the story. It is the feeling of peace he gave through his presence. As my family were assembling to leave, some of my children told me about their time with *"that man"* and they felt a deeper connection too. I asked if anyone recalled his name and no one did. I concluded he must have been an Army Chaplain because the experience was truly spiritual. But one of my sons said it wasn't the chaplain because he had met him. But he was wearing an Army uniform decorated with many ribbons so he had to be an officer. I formed the opinion that he did not introduce himself because it would have been a distraction and he would not have been able to mingle with us as he wanted. Such humility, I believe, is a sign of true greatness. Now I am sure I could play "Dick Tracy" and find out his name, but the thing is, I don't have any desire. The man will remain nameless because it was his love and compassion that led him to come and look grieving families in their eyes filled with tears and walk a few steps with them under their cross. A real modern-day Saint Simon. And because his motivation came from unselfish love, God granted His greatest Gift to be left behind which was *His* Love and Peace. True vocations bring God to the world and all I can say is "Mission accomplished." Whatever our vocation, may we allow God to freely flow from us to our neighbor and thus bring Heaven on earth. That is the gift I received in my heart that day and I am compelled to pass it on to you..

> *"Lord God, our strength and salvation, put in us the flame of Your Love and make our love for You grow to a perfect love which reaches to our neighbor"*(Div Off Vol IV pg 731).

After the Memorial Service there was an outdoor ceremony of the troops marching in formation with the American Flag, front and center, leading the way. Then several officers gave talks congratulating them on a Mission well-done and how proud they were of them all. Then they were dismissed.

The Officers mingled with the families in the bleachers. One in particular, I remember, took out his wallet, as tears filled his eyes, to show me a paper. DJ's name and other soldiers that he had known that gave the ultimate sacrifice. May God soften his memories and give him grace to continue to carry his cross in love and peace.

Then Jarvis Gibson approached to give me a hug and immediately I said,

"I feel DJ in your embrace."

He smiled and with his right arm still around my shoulders he gestured to the soldiers in front of us saying,

"We are all your sons."

I felt God confirmed that Truth deep within my soul.

"Soldiers are your children."

Then he led me down the bleachers to the field to mingle with the soldiers.

Many came to give me a hug and/or shake my hand as they introduced themselves. I, for my part, got to tell them how grateful I was that they were home and thanked them for all they had sacrificed for America. While the crowd began to break open I caught sight of one soldier who was just staring at me. When I realized he was not going to come to me I went to him. As I approached I saw he was not looking at me but DJ's Trinity Cross I wore around my neck. He spoke, still staring at it, *"When I think of DJ, that is all I see and I don't even know what it means."*

"It is the sign of your salvation. A sign of how much God loves you."

"Oh, by the way, I'm SSG Michael Bordes," as we shook hands.

"Oh, my gosh! You were standing right next to DJ!" I dropped his hand to hug him. *"I'm so grateful you didn't get hurt!"*

Later, at the Ball, I gave him *my* Trinity Cross I always had in my car – never knowing DJ had done the same. What a miracle! The first soldier to help DJ... all the fire, blood and gore... and yet his first memory is the Trinity Cross; Father, Son, and Holy Spirit. *(picture and explanation on page 141)* What a special Grace that God has given to Michael. May he pursue God so it may always be so.

Next on the agenda we were given a tour of Charlie Company Headquarters and shown pictures of DJ and 1LT Osbaldo Orozco, assembled together in one frame with their stories – a lasting memorial of their sacrifice.

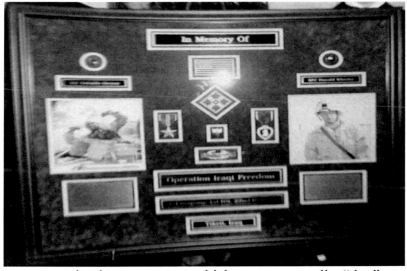

Then a tree planting ceremony which my sons really "dug" – pun intended. Lastly, we went to see the statue made by an Iraqi sculptor. Officers and non-commissioned officers of the 4th Infantry approved a life-size bronze sculpture to honor the dozens of troops the unit had lost in its eleven months in Iraq. They took the bronze from statues outside of Hussein's presidential palace which was used as the 4th Infantry Headquarters in Tikrit, Iraq, DJ's home. There were two statues, 50 foot high, featuring the dictator on galloping horses with his sword raised. *Americans got rid of him and his statues!* Now and forever more at Fort Hood there is a statue of an American Soldier on bended knee, hand covering his eyes in mourning, in front of a Field Cross and behind him a little girl with her hand ready to tap his shoulder to offer him flowers. It is a beautiful depiction reminding everyone that the Iraqi people now have a chance at a better future due to the American Soldiers. It is a reminder that the cost of Freedom is not cheap – A Moment of Death and New Life.

In Tikrit, Iraq then traveled to its home in Fort Hood, Texas
http://www.examiner.com/family-issues-in-national/patricia-walston

PROGRAM FOR THE BALL
C Company
First Battalion
Twenty-Second
Infantry Regiment
Memorial Ball
June 30th, 2004

(inside)

1800 Cocktails	2102 Benediction
1830 Receiving Line	2105 Colors Retired
1900 Colors Posted	2115 Entertainment
1910 Invocation: SPC Steven Perry	**Toasts**
1911 Welcome:	"To the Colors"
CPT Bradley L. Boyd	*Response*: "To the Colors"
Commander, C Co 1-22 INF	"To the President of the United
1915 Grog Ceremony	States"
1930 Toasts	*Response:* "To the Commander-in-Chief"

116

1935 Memorial	"To the Army"
1LT Jason R. Lojka	*Response*: "To the Army"
1945 Promotion Ceremony	"To Fallen Comrades"
2000 Dinner	*Response*: "To LT Orozco and
2100 Closing Remarks	SPC Wheeler"
CPT Bradley L. Boyd	Moment of Silence
(on the back)	**IN MEMORIAM**

1LT OSBALDO OROZCO
Born 19 March 1977 in Earliment, CA. An avid football player and boxing fan. Graduated from Cal Poly San Luis Obispo University and was commissioned through the Army ROTC program where he branched Infantry. Completed the Infantry Officer's Basic Course at Fort Benning, GA and reported to C Co 1st BN 22nd IN RGT and served as 2nd PLT's Platoon Leader. 1LT Orozco was killed in action on the night of 25 April 2003 during a firefight with Iraqi insurgents in northern Cadaseeya.

SPC DONALD WHEELER, JR
Born 15 July 1981 in Concord, MI. Graduated from high school. Enlisted in the Army as an Infantryman immediately following the events of 11 September 2001. Completed Basic Training and Advanced Individual Training at Fort Benning, GA. Reported to C Co 1st BN 22nd IN RGT and initially served as a driver and then as a gunner in 2nd PLT and 1st PLT. SPC Wheeler made the ultimate sacrifice on 13 October 2003 while conducting a combat patrol in Tikrit.

Due to the emotional side of this experience I do not recall all the details but some of the things I do remember are having our picture taken in front of a large brass profile of Hussein, making us feel we participated in his capture;

giving SSG Micheal Bordes *my* Holy Trinity Cross; and then I was approached by a soldier who I thought looked to be in his thirties. He had stood back looking at me until he finally approached. He told me while they were deployed in Cuba he began missing his wife and kids something terrible when DJ offered him his Bible, saying God was the greatest source of comfort he knew. He went on to share:

"DJ had wisdom beyond his years. His faith in God helped me to rediscover my own Catholic Faith. My love for It has been renewed. I wouldn't have made it through that mission in Cuba if it hadn't been for your son." As he spoke tears welled up as he confessed, *"My mother told me to make sure I spoke with you or I would regret it for the rest of my life."*

JULY 15, 2004   DJ'S 23RD BIRTHDAY

I attended 6:45am Mass. The priest, at the consecration, elevated Jesus unusually high, with his head tilted to the heavens causing me to be drawn into a vision. I was allowed to "see" the veil being pulled back which allowed me to penetrated Heaven. I was *led* into the Throne Room of God, the Father. I could see Jesus' Flesh-torn, ripped-opened, unrecognizable Bloodied Body sprawled in front of Abba, Father. Because of my love and compassion that The Father had to witness this horrible scene I cried,

"Oh, what horrible pain! The sight of Your Dead Son!"
I heard, *"What of DJ?"*
Then I let out an audible sob as I leaned on the pew and bowed my head. To have the still, small Voice compare DJ to Jesus seemed sacrilegious, so wrong to even have such a thought. I was humbled and still. I was led further in my thinking,

"What of DJ's death?"
I responded instantly how angry I would be if people were able to witness his sacrifice and no one would bother to take the time to show up! After all he went through and gave up to protect the freedom of people he never knew because he was ordered by our Nation, the United States of America. Boy, everybody had better show up!

In that instant God the Father let me look through *His Eyes.* Then I understood. That is what God The Father is seeing at every Mass. The Father's Son, Jesus Christ, is crucified. Time is irrelevant to God.

"With the Lord a day is like a thousand years, and a thousand years are like a day"(2 Peter 3:8).

118

Every Mass is truly the Life, Death and Resurrection of Jesus Christ, The Pascal Mystery. No reenactment. Eucharist means Thanksgiving. Where are the people? Where is the thanksgiving?

<u>NEVER MISS A CHANCE TO GO TO CHURCH</u>
<u>TO SHOW YOUR LOVE AND GIVE THANKS TO GOD.</u>

DJ 'S MEMORIAL CARDS

For a couple of DJ's anniversaries, I made memorial cards and placed them in the churches where I attended Mass.

THE FRONT

THE LADY OF ALL NATIONS

Lord Jesus Christ, Son of the Father,
send now Your Spirit over the earth. Let the
Holy Spirit live in the hearts of all nations,
that they may be preserved from
degeneration, disaster, and war.
May the Lady of All Nations, who once
was Mary, be our Advocate. Amen.
In this time, Mary wants to be the Lady, the
Mother of All Nations. She appeared under this
title from 1945-1959 to a woman in Amsterdam,
Ida Peerdeman, and gave the above prayer for
the coming of the Holy Spirit over the earth.
The image shows Her as the Co-redemptrix,
Mediatrix, and Advocate standing before the
Cross of Her Son, with whom She was so
intimately and painfully united. Out of Her Hands
stream rays of grace, redemption and peace for
all nations. She may grant these gifts from the
cross to all who say Her prayer daily.

The Lady said:
"This prayer is given for the redemption of the world. This prayer is given for the conversion of the world. Say this prayer in all that you do. You do not know how great and important this prayer is before God. No matter who or what you are, come to the Lady of All Nations."

THE BACK

Donald "DJ" Laverne
Michael Wheeler, JR.
Birth on Earth: July 15, 1981
"I pray for you all every day by saying the rosary. It's the only way to stay sane out here. With all that's happened so far and still to happen."
"Be strong. It will all work out in the end."
July 27, 2003
Birth into Eternal Life:
October 13, 2003
Anniversary of last apparition of <u>Fatima,</u>
The Miracle of the Sun
AN ATTEMPT TO INTERPRET THE "SECRET" OF FATIMA
"The martyrs die in communion with the Passion of Christ, and their death become as one with his. Their life has itself become a Eucharist, part of the mystery of the grain of wheat which in dying yields abundant fruit.

'My Immaculate Heart will triumph.'

This means, the heart that is open to God, purified by contemplation of God, is stronger than guns and weapons of every kind. The Evil One has power in this world, because our freedom continually lets itself be led away from God. The freedom to choose evil no longer has the last word. The Word that does prevail is this:

120

'In the world you will have tribulation, but
take heart; I have overcome the world' *(Jn 16:33).*
The message of Fatima invites us to trust in this promise."
Cardinal Joseph Ratzinger
Prefect of the Congregation for the Doctrine of the Faith
Now Pope Benedict XVI
Pray for all our troops stationed all over the world.
In particular, DJ's comrades in C. Co. 1st BN 22nd INF 4th
INF DIV, such as; Gibson, Velez, Parker, Bordes, Griffith,
Abear, Evans, Speckler, Lucas, and in memory, Orozco.

Then I changed the design. I kept DJ's side the same but put
the prayers Saint Michael the Archangel taught the children on the
other side in order to prepare us for the arrival of Blessed Mary,
Queen of Peace.

BE EVER VIGILANT.
BE PREPARED.
The Angel of Peace prepared
the shepherd children for
the miracle at Fatima. Let
us use the self-same words.
ANGEL OF PEACE PRAYERS

**My God, I believe, I adore, I hope,
and I love You! I ask You for pardon for
those who do not believe, who do not
adore, who do not hope, and who
do not love you."**

ANGEL'S PRAYER

**"MOST HOLY TRINITY;
Father, Son, and Holy Spirit;
I adore Thee profoundly. I offer Thee
the Most Precious Body, Blood,
Soul, and Divinity of Jesus Christ,
present in all the Tabernacles of
the world, in reparation for the
outrages, sacrileges, and indifference
by which He is offended.
And through the infinite merit of His
Most Sacred Heart, and the
Immaculate Heart of Mary,
I beg of Thee the conversion of poor sinners. (3x's)**

CHAPTER NINE: GOD'S MIGHTY HAND

NOVEMBER 2004

At church preparing for Mass I was reviewing the readings for the day from my daily missal. I began to notice the edge of a paper that I randomly placed in it over a year ago. The significance of that paper was its connection to DJ. It was the notes of a homily given at Saint Joseph Catholic Church near Fort Hood, Texas on April 2, 2003, the day before DJ"s deployment. I remembered the Mass was the beginning of Lent. Just looking at it flooded me with memories. *DJ's last day before deploying. Lent.* Our Heavenly Father's Son going into the desert and my son was going into the desert. I could remember feeling humble to think my son and my Savior had something in common. I recalled sharing this with DJ and all the kids. Now he was gone. The edge of the paper flooded me with memories of DJ's last day with me. *Memories.* Memories of his face, his smile, his hugs. I was not crying or angry. Just aware that paper connected me to when DJ was alive. Then a thought, *"Leave it where it is and see if there is a message."* Was I to make a sort-of game out of this piece of paper? It had to be DJ giving me the idea. Okay. What the heck. I'm in no hurry to look at it. Besides, this thought sparked within me a hopeful anticipation. And if it turned out to be nothing I still had my memories.

The day arrived, the last Saturday before Advent. I will copy word for word *"the message"*.

THE VATICAN II WEEKDAY MISSAL
Companion Volume to The Vatican II Sunday Missal
MEDIATION FOR SPIRITUAL GROWTH Page 1609
(HEAVEN) – "For by reason of the fact that those in Heaven are more closely united with Christ, they establish the whole Church more firmly in holiness, lend nobility to the worship which the Church offers to God here on earth and in many ways contribute to its greater edification. For after they have been **received into their heavenly home and are present to the Lord**, through Him and with Him and in Him **they do not cease to intercede with the Father for us**, showing forth the merits which they won on earth through The One Mediator between God and man, serving God in all things and filling up in their flesh those things which are lacking of the sufferings of Christ for His Body which is the Church. **Thus by their brotherly interest our weakness is greatly strengthened.**"
Vatican II, "Constitution on the Church," n. 49

THIS CONFIRMED MY CONFIDENCE THAT DJ DID NOT LEAVE THE MISSION OR HIS BUDDIES AND WILL NEVER LEAVE US.

REMEMBER THIS INCLUDES ALL OUR LOVED ONES. WE PRAY FOR THEM AND THEY PRAY FOR US.

That paper will remain at page 1609 as a reminder of the Mighty Hand of God is in the details of my life. I am forever hope-filled. Thanks be to God!

"It is the Lord Who marches before you; He will be with you and will never fail you or forsake you. So do not fear or be dismayed"(Deut 31:8).

Years later, when the Lord knew my heart was ready, in God's perfect timing, I was *shown* that the readings for that day consummated all that I had grown to understand.

FIRST READING:

"Then the angel showed me the river of life-giving water, sparkling like crystal, flowing from the Throne of God and of the Lamb down the middle of its street. On either side of the River grew the Tree of Life that produces fruit twelve times a year, once each month; the leaves of the Trees serve as Medicine for The Nations. Nothing accursed will be found there anymore. The Throne of God and of The Lamb will be in it, and His servants will worship Him. They will look upon His Face, and His Name will be on their foreheads. Night will be no more, nor will they need light from lamp or sun, for the Lord God shall give them Light, and they shall reign forever and ever." (Revelations 22:1-7)

GOSPEL: EXHORTATION TO BE VIGILANT

"Beware that your hearts do not become drowsy from carousing and drunkenness and the anxieties of daily life, and that day catch you by surprise like a trap. For that day will assault everyone who lives on the face of the earth. Be vigilant at all times and pray that you have the strength to escape the tribulations that are imminent and to stand before the Son of Man." (Luke 21:34-35)

Do you understand? The Mass-The Altar-Jesus' Sacrifice, Body, Blood, Soul, and Divinity flowing over All Nations-Worship and give Glory to God out of Love and do not succumb to lewd behavior and pray, pray, pray.

You with eyes...see. You with ears...*listen.*

Be Watchful, Be Vigilant and Pray, pray, pray constantly.
Are we getting the message?

123

"Let your life be free from love of money but be content with what you have, for he has said, 'I will never forsake you or abandon you.' Thus we may say with confidence: 'The Lord is my helper,[and] I will not be afraid. What can anyone do to me?'" (Heb 13:5-6).

AUGUST 2005

I was signing in for my Adoration Hour when a picture of Blessed Mary on a flier for a pilgrimage to Medugorje caught my eye. This is a town where Blessed Mary has been appearing since 1981, *(the same year DJ was born)*, repeating much the same words spoken at Fatima and giving stern warnings. After praying about it, I signed up along with my four youngest. One of the things we did once we were there was to spend a night on top of Cross Mountain (Krizevac). It was a clear starry night as we picked a spot and settled down. As I was beginning to doze off, I heard someone very excited say,

"Wow! Look at the stars."

I turned on my back and looked up. What I saw broke my heart. One after another, after another, **stars were falling** from the sky. *"Shine on the world like bright stars"*...stars meant lives... souls. And falling meant dying... lost forever.

Yes, my reaction was different from everyone else. Our Lady's pleading was all I could hear,

"Pray. Pray constantly and make sacrifices - for many souls fall into hell like snowflakes because there are none to mortify themselves and to pray for them."

MAY 2006

The dedication of renaming VFW Post #823 and Auxiliary was held on May 21, 2006. The new name is:

DONALD L. WHEELER, JR. Post #823
of the Veterans of Foreign Wars
Jackson, Michigan

We had the privilege of meeting LTC Steve Russell, who flew in for the occasion and honored us with the following words. I spoke a few words, too, since from the very moment of DJ's first heartbeat my intent was for Uncle Don to be remembered. Now because DJ was a man of commitment, truly showing himself to take after his namesake, their name will go down in history as two men who gave the ultimate sacrifice for all of us to have the privilege of living in the Land of Free, the Home of the Brave - The United States of America.

LTC STEVE RUSSELL
VFW POST #823 DEDICATION
SPC DONALD L. WHEELER, JR.

Distinguished guests, fellow veterans, friends, and especially to the family of DJ Wheeler. It means a great deal to come here and participate in the honoring of a great soldier that I had the privilege to serve with in Iraq.

Specialist DJ Wheeler was a great soldier. Not because he is gone and we try to remember him kindly, but because he was truly a great soldier. Wheeler had an easy-going style and confidence. He was good with people. He was good at his job. He knew his weapons and how to follow orders, but more importantly, his peers seemed to defer to him. Deferred leadership is the most powerful kind because it is usually given to an individual solely as a result of having earned the respect of others. They looked up to him. I wish I had hundreds of him. That is why his loss was felt so deeply by all of us.

A day does not go by that I do not think about the soldiers I commanded and those that did not come home with us. In October, 2003 in Tikrit, Iraq, I said goodbye to Wheeler and another soldier named James Edward Powell that died about 12 hours before DJ. As we paid our respects, we pledged that as long as we have breath, we should never forget them. That is why a dedication such as this one means so much to us and for that we all say, *"Thank you."*

My words at the dedication to honor my son.

Thank you to all who have come to honor DJ, SPC Donald L. Wheeler, Jr. I want to recognize two of my sons, Paul and Quentin, who have enlisted into the Army and three other sons with their eyes on the Military.

The idea of renaming this Post was brought to my attention by Michael O'Keefe who was seeking my permission to proceed with this project. I was deeply moved and humbled. Then the reality that the Lord had put in place another Michael – this one being the sixth and I am even more confident that God is in the details of my life.

1.) Confirmation – Michael would protect DJ all his life and after joining the Army, after 9-11, I knew they would be victorious over the evil that hit our world.

2.) October 13, 2003 when the officer came to tell us of DJ's sacrifice, I heard the still, small Voice to ask him for his first name – another Michael. It was then that I had immediate calm and peace and strength to carry on.

3.) The Bradley that DJ drove had his Trinity Crucifix hanging in it but on the day of his birth into Eternal Life he was in another Bradley that was in the care of a soldier named Michael.

125

4.) We learned months later, like gathering pieces to a puzzle, that during the attack of 2 RPG's the soldier standing next to DJ was another Michael. I met this Michael while I was wearing the Trinity Crucifix around my neck and he kept staring at It. I had an exact replica in my car – unaware that DJ was looking at one every day, too – so I gave this Michael mine. I am confident that God will soften any lasting troubling memories of his deployment and replace them with His Mercy and Grace as long as his heart remains open to God.

5.) The soldier who prepared DJ's body to leave Tikrit was also a Michael.

Several men of great physical strength but their greatest strength is their love and compassion for their fellowman.

When Michael O'Keefe told me he was having a Flag made with DJ's name on it to represent their Post #823 he triggered another memory in this journey as mom to DJ. Watching DJ raise the Flag at Fort Hood, Texas, tears fell because it felt sacred. Then afterward DJ told me that they were complimented by an officer who had been in the Army for decades saying he had never witnessed the Flag handled with so much reverence and respect. I knew what he meant. I told DJ, *"I know one day the Flag will be honoring you."* as I hugged him.

I didn't know what I meant then but I do now. When I saw my son's coffin draped by the Flag - realizing It had covered DJ all the way from Tikrit until it arrived here in Michigan. The Flag took over my job as mother - embracing, protecting and alerting all who looked to show my son honor and respect. As he was wheeled to the hearse we processed behind but I had to walk faster so as to touch the Flag – my way of thanking It for honoring DJ.

Then I had a clearer understanding of the symbolism of the Flag. Stars represent soldiers lives; the red and white stripes represent their blood, sweat and tears... their all. And as the Flag waves, their sacrifice continues to wash over all of us. The Flag is sacred. May we never forget all the Veterans who gave their all. I have another Flag that all DJ's buddies signed while still in Iraq. *(two of my kids unfolded it)* This one filled with personal words of remembrance means the world to us and more especially to DJ.

My son's very name came from a deep desire of mine. A man, SGT Donald L. Wheeler, served during the Korean War conflict and at the age of 23 he gave his all. Only thing I had ever heard about him was that he loved kids but never had the chance to have any of his own. I felt his sacrifice could not go unnoticed. Which brings us to this great day. Now because of DJ, SPC Donald L. Wheeler, Jr., his Great Uncle, SGT Donald Wheeler, is being honored, too. **MAY WE NEVER FORGET.** I am humbled at the privilege to witness this occasion and I am confident they both are smiling.

In closing I want you to know DJ wrote home saying,

"the only way to stay sane over here is by saying the rosary." Through his prayers he was able to keep strong and confident in his love for God and more importantly God's love for him – reassuring DJ he was not alone. DJ wrote that he could feel the very Presence of God and through DJ's words I was led to Saint Paul's Letter to the Philippians. I challenge all of you to read it. Open your mind and open your heart and allow the Holy Spirit to fill you. He can change your life.

Commit yourself to pray, to sacrifice and do penance, and repent of past sins and *listen* to God. Remember, if we want to change the world and truly honor the memory of DJ and Uncle Don and all the Veterans who gave their all, it starts with us. Let us be people of commitment and change our world! Thank you and may God Bless America.

NOVEMBER 2008

The week began, Sunday, November 2, during my prayers and worship of our God with a beautiful phrase that kept flowing into my thoughts, *"The Mighty Hand of God."* I agreed with the idea that God's Hand was indeed Mighty and I found joy in being reminded. Then on Tuesday I received a phone call from a very excited daughter, a nursing student at college.

"Mom, you won't believe who I met!"

"Well, tell me."

"No, I'm on my way home. I want to tell you in person. You just won't believe it!"

"Well, be careful driving. I can't wait to hear."

A couple of hours later she came bursting into the house and began her story. *"I was doing my clinicals*(a class that is on the job training) *and we were allowed to pick our patient so I picked a woman named Mary. You and Blessed Mary so I figured this "Mary" would be good, too. When I got to the room a man was there but I wanted to keep my mind on the patient. This was counting as a grade so I needed to gather all her information. The man said something and I heard the word 'Army' but I did not want to start talking personal stuff so I kept my focus on the patient. Then a couple of more times I heard him mention Army and then heard Tikrit, Iraq. Well, with that I had to speak about DJ dying in Tikrit. Then he said, 'DJ Wheeler?' I nodded. He said, 'I was his doctor.' He said he would never forget that day because of the love he felt from DJ's buddies and that he felt for him, too, even though they had never met. And so when he got back in the States he found DJ's picture in a magazine and has carried it with him ever since."*

I couldn't believe it. Oh, my, gosh! God's Mighty Hand was at work. This was evidence of it. I wanted to meet him. I *had* to meet him to shake his hand for trying to save my son. She had clinicals

127

again on Friday so it was already set-up to meet Dr. Robert. I couldn't wait!

Friday finally arrived and when the introductions, hand shaking and hugs were over he shared,

"I never discuss my Army career with anyone. So every time I would open my mouth and share something about my career with your daughter I was kicking myself inside to shut-up! She doesn't care. Then I would say something more and I would reprimand myself to knock it off. Finally the third time when I said I served in Tikrit, Iraq - she said that is where her brother died, I just blurted out, 'DJ Wheeler?' And she said yes. Then it all made sense."

"What do you mean it all made sense?"

"Normally I don't come to Michigan this time of year. I usually I go fishing with my buddies. I really didn't have a good excuse to give my buddies why I wasn't going with them other than I just had to come to Michigan to visit my Mom."

"The Mighty Hand of God. He put you two in the right place at the right time so we could have further knowledge that He has not let go of us – these five years later. To continue Trusting Him. And I do."

THANK YOU, GOD!

Then the next day I got a phone call from my son deployed in Iraq, first one back into that country since DJ.

"Mom, a funny thing happened yesterday."

"Oh, good. I like funny stories. What's yours?"

"We got bombed while we were in our tent but no one got hurt. We were all knocked out of our cots and it was a real mess but no one was hurt!"

"Praise God! But that's not a funny story."

Then we lost the connection. It was a good thing, too, because my hand started shaking, then my body and then tears were filling my eyes. I handed my phone to one of my sons and said, *"If he calls back tell him I have gone to light a candle out of gratitude to God, that His Mighty Hand protected him."*

I laid myself on the floor in front of the Altar at Church out of deep humility realizing how much God loves us. God is in the details of our lives. ***The Mighty Hand of God.***

NOVEMBER 2009

I had changed parishes. My pastor had been reassigned and the parish was only a five to ten minute extra driving time so I decided to make the sacrifice. He was my shepherd, after-all, and like an obedient lamb, I followed.

This new drive had me passing a business that had a magnificent display of the American Flag. It made me feel every time I drove by like I was on a military base *(at that point I had four sons in the Army and as I write this I have six)*. My way to show the Flag my highest respect is by making the Sign of the Cross because it represents sacrifice. As DJ's 6th Anniversary was approaching, I felt DJ was telling me to thank them for their Flag. Being a shy person I was not too anxious to fulfill this inspiration. But I did begin to notice where the main office door was and began imagining myself walking through it – my way of building up my courage. Finally by Veteran's Day – yes, almost a whole month later – I bought a wreath for the upcoming Holiday season and stopped.

As I walked through the office door, there was a customer about ready to leave, a tall man behind the counter, and a woman at a desk behind him. The customer changed his mind when he saw me and said smiling, *"I'm not going anywhere. I have to hear what this is all about,"* and stepped aside.

I addressed the man behind the counter, *"May I speak with the owner?"*

"That would be me. How can I help you?"

Laying the wreath on his counter I continued, *"I am Marycay Wheeler. I am a mother of four sons in the Army and two are deployed, one in Afghanistan and one in Iraq, and every time I go by here I feel like I am on an Army base."* With my voice quivering and tears filling my eyes, I continued as I noticed the man's eyes were beginning to fill with tears.

"My son, SPC Donald L Wheeler, Jr, sixth anniversary of his death in Iraq was just last month and I felt he was urging me to stop and thank you for your Flag."

"May I give you a hug?"

Now it was my turn to be surprised as I nodded. As he came around the counter and faced me he said, *"It was because of your son I put the Flag up."*

Then I cried as we hugged. I thanked him and he thanked me for my son, DJ, and all my sons' patriotism. As I made my way to leave, my knees were weak. As I got in my car the floodgates opened up and I sobbed. I was confirmed in the fact that my son, DJ, was with me and still was prodding me on in my Faith and Trust in God – Joy in the Cross!

THANK YOU, STEINKE-FENTON FABRICATORS, INC.
JACKSON, MICHIGAN

IMPORTANT NOTE: The name of the parish that I joined –
OUR LADY OF FATIMA.

As a member of Our Lady of Fatima I volunteered to enhance their daily prayer booklet. As I typed the prayers and reread them for typos, I discovered the word "army" in one of the prayers. I thought with six of my sons joining the Army it was infiltrating all areas of my life. The soldiers, not only my sons, were always in my prayers and here was the proof! So as I read the prayer more closely to see what word I really meant to type I discovered I meant to type the word, "Mary." I was so excited, I immediately emailed my sons. They knew about Fatima and the Blue Army and the blue cord being the Infantry's color but this new reality that the very word "Army" was also the most blessed Name of "Mary". Mary and Army were one and the same - **AN UNBEATABLE TEAM!**

NOVEMBER 2010

With the deployment of my fifth son, third son in Iraq, I received an email and here is how it unfolded:

Ma'am,   November 18, 2010

My name is Roland Hale. I'm an Army journalist serving in Iraq with your son's unit. I talked to him last week regarding my interest in doing a story about his fallen brother, your son. I understand that this is a very personal subject, but I also think that this story deserves to be told. Would you mind answering a few questions I have for this? I can try to reach you by phone, or I can email you my questions. Thank you very much for your help.   Respectfully, SPC Roland Hale

Dear SPC Hale,   November 30, 2010

I have been away from my computer for these last many days and this is the first time I have gotten to answer my emails. Yes, Dominic mentioned you would be contacting me. If I can be of assistance I will try. Thank you for your service to our country.

God bless all our troops.   Marycay

Ma'am,   December 1, 2010

Thanks for your reply. No worries. I know how it is to be busy! Happy holidays to you, as well. I just have a few questions for my story. Please don't feel obligated to answer any that you are not comfortable with. *(Here are some of the questions since many were repeating facts already covered in the previous pages of this book).*

1.) Has your loss been easier to deal with with time?
Because of my belief in God and being Catholic I participate in daily Mass and receive the Sacrament of Reconciliation weekly if not daily, so to be open to God's Grace and Mercy I am working on trying to live up to DJ's words that he wrote from Iraq, *"I say the rosary every day, It is the only way to stay sane out here. With all that happens so far and still to happen... but stay STRONG. IT WILL ALL WORK OUT IN THE END."* That was written in July, 2003. So with God's Grace I carry on and I hope DJ is proud of me.

2.) Did the military history of the family make the loss harder, easier?
It made me aware of how many other American families have had to sacrifice for our country over the years. It made me feel very close to them - A BIG FAMILY. Our hearts forever united. I wanted to do whatever I could to help other families so I tried to get a job on any military base. I would clean toilets or babysit - anything. Just so I could help relieve some of their burdens. *(My sons' recruiter could not find a place for me.)* Nothing sadder to see than the children having to say good-bye to their daddy or mommy. It tears your heart out, as you well know. So I pray. That, too, is a real weapon, as DJ confessed.

3.) Have you had any apprehension about Dominic joining/serving in Iraq?
I was once asked if I hated the Iraqi's. "No." What I do hate are people who think they should have the power to take what each human being has a right to by God and that is their FREEDOM. I am humbled at the courage my son, Dominic, shows by carrying on with the Mission to keep the Iraqi people FREE. I raised my sons to be men, not boys, and if they feel God is calling them to serve in the Military to protect our Nation during a time of war, I am humbled and proud to be their mother.

4.) How close was Dominic with his brother?
DJ was born in '81 and Dominic '91. DJ was a good big brother. I will let Dominic's own words answer this question: When we were down at Fort Hood, Texas, April, 2003, seeing DJ deployed into Iraq I had a moment alone with Dominic, 11 years old at the time, and asked him how he felt about DJ going off to war. And his response, with immediate tears, was, *"Just as long as he comes home."*

5.) How important was it to you, the family, when Dominic flew the flag over Tikrit?
DJ's blood lies in the ground of that country and it is sacred to me. And to know that one of my sons got to be close to that hallowed ground, it filled my heart - hard to express.

6.) Do you think that flying the flag was a form of personal closure for Dominic, or did it also give a sense of closure to you and the family?

To see the area that was the last scene that DJ saw... very sacred. Dominic took several pictures. I am sure Dominic can speak for himself on how it felt for him. One day I, too, will visit and walk the area. With all my five Army soldiers at my side in honor of DJ's sacrifice. He knows we know where he fell and where his blood left his body. Yes, someday...

7.) Does Dominic still have the flag with him, or has he given it to you?

Dominic still has it, which tells you how he feels about the honor.

8.) Do you feel a sense of bitterness or of resentment at the military or the government for your son's death?

Iraqi's deserve to know FREEDOM. It is God-given. I will forever miss my son. I am proud to be his mother and realizing that when he saw something as horrible as 9-11, he did not wait for someone else to do something. He wanted to help prevent it ever happening again. Bin Laden and Hussein and others like them need to be stopped. And by the way, it was DJ's buddies who helped find the hole that snake, Hussein, was hiding in on December 13, 2003, two months after DJ's birth into Eternal Life. Just my thought: DJ gave them the location because he had a better view of the situation. Because I again believe that he will never leave the Mission. No RIP, rest in peace, but FOREVER VIGILANT.

9.) Does the family support the wars in Iraq and Afghanistan?

Terrorists will be forever a part of how we live and we must keep them from getting into a position of reforming so to build up to the strength they had after Clinton failed as a Commander in Chief during the Mogadishu /Somalia, East Africa incident: "Black Hawk Down". ALL Nations saw our soldiers being dragged through the streets and; *(well, words cannot clearly describe what those soldiers went through and then to think of those families who saw their sons being treated that way)*; We, the United States of America did nothing. NOTHING?!!! That is when I feel Bin Laden and Hussein and all "evil" leaders saw U.S. as weak.

If we are making some kind of progress, then good. I must trust the ones on the ground. I know regular media is not a good source of news. So I must trust those in charge of my sons and all the troops.

I will continue to Trust in God and pray for His intervention. And I also trust that DJ and all the other soldiers who have given the ultimate sacrifice will not leave the MISSION until it has been accomplished.

And it would be wise to revisit the life of Saint Joan of Arc who, when in charge of leading men into battle, first insisted they did not swear and never ever use God's Name in vain. We have to take responsibility for our own actions if we want God to fight alongside of US.

Pray with me: *"Angels and Saints, take the Land!"* I find great peace and strength in this prayer and so I know it is of God. And I trust in DJ's own words, too, *"Be STRONG. It'll all work out in the end."* And remember a

132

man is strongest when he is on his knees.

Here is a link to my finished story: *December 13, 2010*
                                                            (Notice the day!!!)
http://www.dvidshub.net/news/61850/soldier-honors-fallen-brother-iraq
I hope that my work can do your family's story justice. At least a little.
Thanks for all of your help. Happy holidays!
                                                            Respectfully, SPC Hale

An Army Black Hawk helicopter passes over Tikrit, Iraq, October 13, 2010 giving PFC Dominic Wheeler, 19, a chance to fly a flag over the spot where his brother, DJ Wheeler, 22, was struck and killed by a rocket propelled grenade in 2003.*(Look closely and you will see the Flag.)*(Photo by U.S. Army)

CAMP TAJI, Iraq –
        "When 11-year-old Dominic Wheeler watched his brother DJ leave for Iraq in 2003, his mother asked how he felt about his brother going to war. "Just as long as he comes home," Dominic responded.
        Seven months into his deployment DJ was killed on patrol when a group of insurgents fired several rocket propelled grenades into his Bradley fighting vehicle. He came home to be buried in Concord, Michigan. But the story did not end there for Dominic. On the seventh anniversary of DJ's death he had a unique opportunity to pay tribute to his brother. Dominic, now 19, is serving with the Army in Iraq as an aviation operations specialist. His unit, the 1st Squadron, 6th Cavalry Regiment, a helicopter unit from

Fort Riley, Kansas, regularly flies missions in the area where DJ was killed.

Soldiers occasionally bring flags on missions to take home as combat keepsakes and the unit gave Dominic the chance to fly a flag for his brother. The flags are usually tucked into a cockpit or crew bag but the unit arranged to allow Dominic to personally unfurl the flag over the city. On October 13, one of the unit's Black Hawk helicopters made a small detour with Dominic aboard. Near the same street where DJ fell, Dominic and one of the crew members spread the flag across the open door of the helicopter. They flew especially low while Dominic held the flag. "It was pretty cool, I was lucky to do it," said Dominic. "None of my brothers have been able to do something like this for DJ."

Dominic kept the flag with him, but sent home word about his experience. The news was particularly important to Dominic's mother, Marycay Thorrez-Wheeler.

"DJ's blood lies in the ground of that country," wrote Marycay in an email, "and to know that one of my sons got to be close to that hallowed ground it filled my heart."

Marycay hopes to visit the spot herself with the rest of DJ's brothers, five of whom are also serving in the Army, she said. "One day I'll walk the area with all my soldiers at my side in honor of DJ's sacrifice."

Her sons will likely be called to serve in combat again, however, before they can re-unite to pay their respects to DJ in Iraq. Four of the five have already served combat tours, and another will possibly deploy to Afghanistan next year. Dominic will return to Fort Riley when his unit completes its year-long tour here."

TRIBUTE: THE MONUMENT AT WITHINGTON PARK aka VETERANS PARK IN JACKSON, MICHIGAN.

After much dedication and hard work by some very wonderful people from our city of Jackson, Michigan – Kelly Trudell, Tina Terry and LTC Curt Lapham, to name a few – a monument was erected. A Fallen Hero's Memorial Concert was held to raise some of the money. I gave a talk while pictures were shown of my sons in the Army and the pictures of the snake hole Saddam Hussein was found in while DJ's buddies held the American Flag over it so as to declare the victory. My youngest son *(who had just enlisted)* held the Flag Case containing DJ's Flag, medals, and Crucifix from his funeral.

The Monument to honor the Soldiers who gave the Ultimate Sacrifice for **THE WAR ON TERROR** was dedicated on November 11, 2010

Donald L. Wheeler Jr.

Brent E. Beeler

Matthew R. Soper

James S. Collin Jr.

I visited the site the day before the big ceremony to take in the significance of the event without all the noise. I strolled the circular sidewalk. In prayerful gratitude I slowly read name after name from all the wars who gave the ultimate sacrifice for me, an American citizen. Then I arrived at the Korean War Monument and found, third from the bottom, Uncle Don's name, SGT Donald L. Wheeler. I turned and looked behind me. Their war monuments were across from each other!

UNCLE DON AND DJ

BROUGHT TOGETHER BY NAME,

MEMORIALIZED FOR LIFE,

LIVING OUT ETERNITY IN HEAVEN.

GOD IS GOOD!

This is the view from the
War on Terror Monument.
Korean Monument is straight
ahead, behind the flag pole

"Dedicated to those who followed
in the paths taken by earlier
patriots and offered their lives in
service to their country during
the Global War on Terror.

Because of them
  - we are free
  - our nation lives
  - our world is blessed"

Pictures by Faith Draper: examiner.com

136

TRIBUTE: SGT DONALD L. WHEELER, UNCLE DON

IN GRATEFUL MEMORY OF

SERGEANT DONALD L. WHEELER

WHO DIED IN THE SERVICE OF HIS COUNTRY

**in the military operations in Korea
on September 20, 1950**

HE STANDS IN THE UNBROKEN LINE OF
PATRIOTS WHO HAVE DARED TO DIE
THAT FREEDOM MIGHT LIVE AND GROW
AND INCREASE ITS BLESSINGS. FREEDOM LIVES, AND
THROUGH IT, HE LIVES--IN A WAY THAT HUMBLES THE
UNDERTAKINGS OF MOST MEN.

HARRY TRUMAN
PRESIDENT OF THE UNITED STATES OF AMERICA

KOREAN MONUMENT: UNCLE DON, THIRD NAME FROM THE BOTTOM, ACROSS FROM DJ.

DREAMS RECALLED

I would not say I have had an abundance of dreams of DJ but just the opposite. But they have been encouraging or a serious wake-up call. Here's a couple.

1) With my children around me, in a home setting, DJ appeared in BDU and looked at me and said,

"No rest for the wicked means no rest for the righteous, Mom."

2) Saw DJ in battle gear walking in a strong confident stride heading up a mountain. (One son deployed in Afghanistan while another was preparing to be deployed.)

3) DJ in shorts and tee shirt like Army soldiers wear for PT's. He was sitting, leaning forward with his elbows on his knees, breathing heavily and looking at the ground as water dripped off him. When I woke, I thought it meant he had just finished a run but I was led to realize it was connected to a previous dream where I was alone in the ocean with sharks circling all around me. When the first one attacked I struck him with my fist which actually made me wake up when my arm hit the bed. I understand that DJ was all wet and exhausted because he was constantly helping me in my struggles in life. I prayed for the courage to face my struggles in life so DJ could continue to concentrate all his energy on the welfare of all soldiers.

WEDNESDAY, APRIL 27, 2011

I was sharing with a friend that two of my sons were going to be deployed in Afghanistan. The first one arrived in early April and the other would be arriving in early June. I TRUSTED that Good would prevail. After saying this I *"saw"* an Angel on a mountaintop holding his sword and shield high in the air in Victory. I began to cry because I knew it was Saint Michael. When I got home and walked into my living room I saw DJ's statue from his confirmation. Though the hair and clothes were different color I felt confident that what I *"saw"* was indeed the TRUTH. Victory was soon to be realized.

SUNDAY, MAY 1, 2011

Bin Laden is dead. Praise the Lord! I danced as I heard the news. Another modern-day Hitler is gone. All due to the great heroism of our military and great sacrifices of military families. Glory to God for allowing Saint Michael and the Angels and all the Saints to aid these courageous and vigilant men and women of the U.S. military.

I have been overwhelmed by God's assurance that He allowed Saint Michael the Archangel to be forever vigilant when it was about my son.

1.) The soldier who brought the news of DJ's birth into Eternal Life was Michael.
2.) The soldier who stood beside DJ in the Bradley when he died was Michael.
3.) The soldier whose Bradley DJ was in was a Michael *(DJ's Bradley had his Fatima Holy Trinity Cross hanging in it. Last vision seen by Sister Lucia, the eldest visionary, on June 13, 1929 explained on page 141.)*
4.) The soldier that zipped DJ into his body bag when he left Tikrit, Iraq was Michael.
5.) An elderly veteran that came to my son's funeral and has been supportive to me ever since; his Confirmation name is Michael.
6.) The veteran who was the driving force behind the VFW building named in DJ's and Uncle Don's honor, on May 21, 2006, was Michael.

CHAPTER TEN : RELIGIOUS UNDERSTANDING OF THE "ULTIMATE SACRIFICE"

The blood of soldiers that have given the ultimate sacrifice, *their all,* for their country is mingled with the Blood of Christ and presented to God, the Father, in reparation for all the sins the world commits. This belief comes directly from the Mother of God, Blessed Virgin Mary, when She spoke in Fatima, Portugal, to the three shepherd children and the explanation that follows come from the Prefect of the Congregation for the Doctrine of the Faith Cardinal Joseph Ratzinger, now Pope Benedict XVI .

"The martyrs die in communion with the Passion of Christ and their death becomes as one with His. Their life has itself become a Eucharist,part of the mystery of the grain of wheat which in dying yields abundant fruit.

'MY IMMACULATE HEART WILL TRIUMPH.'

This means, the heart that is open to God, purified by contemplation of God, is stronger than guns and weapons of every kind. The evil one has power in this world, because our freedom continually lets itself be led away from God. The freedom to choose evil no longer has the last word. The Word that does prevail is this:

'In the world you will have tribulation, but take heart; I have overcome the world'(John 16:33).**"**

Sister Lucia, the eldest of the three shepherd children from Fatima experienced more visions and I wish to mention two. The Trinity Cross *(DJ hung in his Bradley refer to on page 112-115)* with Blessed Mary and the Eucharist by Jesus' opened side on the left and words on the right, "Grace and Mercy." Along with the vision she received three messages. The first gave her an understanding about the Mystery of the Trinity. The second was to tell the pope and bishops to consecrate Russia to Blessed Mary's Immaculate Heart so to stop the spreading of its errors throughout the world which are materialism, atheism and individualism, putting self before others – all signs of spiritual sickness. Third was a warning of God's Justice to souls who commit sins against Blessed Mary and to sacrifice and make reparation to help these souls. In the other vision Sister Lucia was given a formula on how Jesus wants His Mother to be honored. Now remember God Who needs *nothing* choose to come into the world through Blessed Mary's Womb. We must listen!

Blessed Mary with the Child Jesus suspended upon a cloud Her hand was on His Shoulder and in Her hand was Her Immaculate Heart with thorns wrapped around It. Jesus spoke saying we are to make acts of reparation to remove the thorns put on the Immaculate Heart of our Mother by ungrateful men at every moment. Then Blessed Mary spoke about the men who blaspheme Her and show no gratitude. She then promised to assist at the moment of death with Grace all those who, with the intention of love for Her, fulfill these requests:

1.) For 5 consecutive 1st Saturdays attend Mass
2.) Go to Confession
3.) Receive Holy Communion
4.) Recite 5 decades of the Rosary and
5.) Keep Her company for 15 minutes while meditating on the Mysteries of the rosary with the intention of making reparation to Blessed Mary.

The Lord listed 5 types of offenses and blasphemies against the Immaculate Heart of Mary when people deny:

1.) The Immaculate Conception
2.) Blessed Mary's Virginity
3.) Blessed Mary's Divine Maternity and as the Mother of us all
4.) Set examples of indifference or hatred of Blessed Mary
5.) The desecration against Blessed Mary's holy images (May 29, 1930)

"PRAY, PRAY, PRAY."

"Without unceasing prayer, you cannot experience the beauty and greatness of the Grace which God is offering you"
(Blessed Mary, Medugorje February 25, 1989).

HOW TO PRAY THE ROSARY

1.) Make the "Sign of the Cross" then with fingers on the Crucifix pray the "Apostles Creed".
2.) Pray the "Our Father" on large bead.

3.) Pray three "Hail Mary's" on next 3 smaller beads for an increase of Faith, Hope and Charity.

4.) Pray the "Glory Be" on the space before the next large bead.

5.) Announce the First Mystery then pray the "Our Father" on large bead.

6.) Next ten small beads pray 10 "Hail Mary's".

7.) Pray "Glory Be" and "O my Jesus" on space before large bead.
"O my Jesus, forgive us our sins, save us from the fire of hell, take all souls into Heaven and help especially those most in need of Your mercy."

8.) Announce second Mystery and pray the "Our Father" on large bead.

9.) Repeat steps 6 and 7 and continue with Third, Fourth, and Fifth Mystery.

10.) Pray: **"Hail Holy Queen"; Mother of Mercy, our life, our sweetness and our hope! To Thee do we cry, poor banished children of Eve; to Thee do we send up our sighs, mourning and weeping in this valley of tears. Turn then, most gracious Advocate, Thine Eyes of Mercy toward us, and after this our exile, show unto us the blessed Fruit of Thy Womb, Jesus. O clement, O loving, O sweet Virgin Mary! Pray for us, O Holy Mother of God. That we may be made worthy of the promises of Christ.**

Let us pray: **O God, whose only begotten Son, by His Life, Death, and Resurrection, has purchased for us the rewards of eternal life, grant, we beseech Thee, that meditating upon these Mysteries of the Most Holy Rosary of the Blessed Virgin Mary, we may imitate what they contain and obtain what they promise, through the same Christ our Lord. Amen.**

11.) Say the Our Father, Hail Mary, and Glory Be for the Pope's intentions.

12.) Make the Sign of the Cross.

THE MYSTERIES To pray the rosary while meditating on the Mysteries I use the same booklet DJ used: **"Pray the Rosary" by Rev J. M. Lelen.**

JOYFUL MYSTERY: Prayed on Monday, Saturday and the Sundays of Christmas season.

1.) **Annunciation.** *I desire the love of humility.* Think of the humility of the Blessed Virgin when the Angel Gabriel greeted Her with these words: *"Hail full of Grace."*

2.) **Visitation.** *I desire charity toward my neighbor.* Think of Bl Mary's charity in visiting Her cousin, Elizabeth and remains with her for three months before the birth of Saint John the Baptist.

3.) **Nativity.** *I desire the love of God.* The poverty so lovingly accepted by Bl Mary when She placed the Infant Jesus, our God and Redeemer, in a manger in the stable in Bethlehem.

4.) **The Presentation.** *I desire a spirit of sacrifice.* Think of Bl Mary's obedience to the Law of God in presenting the Child Jesus in the Temple.

5.) **Finding in the Temple.** *I desire zeal for the Glory of God.* Think of the deep sorrow with which Bl Mary sought the Child Jesus for three days, and the joy with which She found Him in the midst of the teachers in the Temple.

LUMINOUS MYSTERY: Thursday

1.) **Baptism of Jesus.** *I desire to live my baptismal promises.* Think of Christ's Baptism at the hands of Saint John the Baptist when the Father called Him His beloved Son and the Holy Spirit descended on Him to invest Him with the Mission He was to carry out.

2.) **Miracle at the wedding in Cana.** *I desire to do whatever Jesus says.* Think of Christ's self-manifestation at the wedding at Cana when He changed water into wine and opened the hearts of His disciples to faith, thanks to the intervention of Bl Mary, the first among believers.

3.) **Proclamation of the Kingdom of God.** *I desire God's forgiveness.* Think of Christ's preaching of the Kingdom of God and its call to forgiveness, as He inaugurated the Ministry of Mercy, which He continues to exercise until the end of the world particularly through the Sacrament of Reconciliation.

4.) **The Transfiguration of Jesus.** *I desire to be a new person in Christ.* Think of Christ's Transfiguration when the Glory of the Godhead shone forth from His Face as the Father commanded the Apostles to **listen to Him** and experience His Passion and Resurrection and be transfigured by the Holy Spirit.

5.) **Institution of the Eucharist.** *I desire active participation at Mass.* Think of Christ's institution of the Eucharist, in which He offered His Body, Blood, Soul and Divinity, under the signs of bread and wine and testified to His love for humanity, for whose sake He would offer Himself in Sacrifice.

SORROWFUL MYSTERY: Tuesday, Friday and the Sundays of Lent

1.) **Agony in the Garden.** *I desire true repentance for my sins.* Think of our Lord Jesus in the Garden of Gethsemani suffering a bitter agony for our sins.

2.) **Scourging at the Pillar.** *I desire a spirit of mortification.* Think of the cruel scourging at the pillar that our Lord suffered at the heavy blows that tore His Flesh.

3.) **Crowning with Thorns.** *I desire moral courage.* Think of the crown of sharp thorns that was forced upon our Lord's Sacred Head and the patience with which He endured the pain for our sins.

4.) **Carrying of the Cross.** *I desire the virtue of patience.* Think of the heavy Cross so willingly carried by our Lord and ask Him to help you to carry your crosses without complaint.

5.) **The Crucifixion.** *I desire the Grace of final perseverance.* Think of the love which filled Christ's Sacred Heart during His three hour agony on the Cross and ask Him to be with you at the hour of death.

GLORIOUS MYSTERY: Wednesday, Sunday.

1.) **The Resurrection.** *I desire a strong faith.* Think of Christ's glorious triumph when on the third day after His Death He arose from the tomb and for forty days appeared to His Bl Mother and to His disciples.

2.) **The Ascension.** *I desire the virtue of hope.* Think of the Ascension of Jesus Christ, forty days after His glorious Resurrection, in the presence of Bl Mary and His disciples.

3.) **The Descent of the Holy Spirit.** *I desire zeal for the Glory of God.* Think of the descent of the Holy Spirit upon Bl Mary and the Apostles, under the form of Tongues of Fire, in the fulfillment of Christ's promise.

4.) **The Assumption.** *I desire the Grace of a holy death.* Think of the glorious Assumption of Bl Mary into Heaven when She was united with Her Divine Son.

5.) **The Coronation of the Blessed Virgin Mary.** *I desire a greater love for Bl Mary.* Think of the glorious crowning of Bl Mary as Queen of Heaven by Her Divine Son, to the great joy of all the Saints.

THE LESSONS LEARNED FROM BEING DJ'S MOM.

Our Lady at Fatima: *"Offer it up because your Heavenly Father is already greatly offended."*

Little Jacinta, Francisco and Lucia helped me, while DJ was in my womb, to change my feelings about pain, emotional suffering, and being afraid.

Our Lady of All Nations:
"...Let the Holy Spirit live in the hearts of all nations..."

My desire:
Set us on fire for love of You, Lord, so to spread to our neighbors so true peace will reign through devotion to the Sacred Heart of Jesus and the Immaculate Heart of Mary.

"I have come to light a fire on the earth.
How I wish the blaze was ignited" (Lk 12:49).

The walls of Jericho came crashing down because Joshua listened and followed God's directions to march behind the Ark of the Covenant – Old Testament type prefiguring Bl Mary *(Josh 6:1-7, Heb 11:30)*. Bl Mary has the directions for Peace and we must listen and follow them. It may seem impossible for man but nothing is impossible for God.

Keeping my eyes on Jesus in Adoration, going to Mass daily, constantly try to change my sinful ways by going to Confession. This is how I have been able to find my way. The heart rendering scene of the Crucifixion of Jesus with His Mother, Bl Mary, standing ever vigilant with Her eyes fixated on Him is a clue how we should act when the cross comes into our lives. Jesus persevered even when He was scourged to the point that His very Bones of His Precious Body were exposed. And *then* He carried The Cross. What we endure doesn't come close to that! Offering it all up to God, The Father, as an act of reparation for all the offenses we, His children, do. Do it with Joy!

"God loves a cheerful giver" (2 Cor 9:7).

"Don't mumble and complain" (Phil 2:14).

"His ways are not our ways" (Is 55:8).

So we should not be surprised when we do not understand. Keep on and carry your cross with joy and total trust. As Saint Augustine speaking to our heavenly Father reminds us:

"You have made us for Yourself, O Lord, and our hearts are restless until they rest in You" (Saint Augustine).

MAY GOD BE PRAISED AND GLORIFIED THROUGH MY SHARING THE WORDS OF MY SON, DJ, A SOLDIER IN THE UNITED STATES ARMY, BUT MORE IMPORTANTLY A SOLDIER FOR CHRIST.

AUTHOR'S BACKGROUND

A strong foundation was laid at the beginning of my life due to my parents, who gave me the gift of baptizing me, Mary Catherine Thorrez, and raising me Roman Catholic. The source of all true and perfect gifts flow from the Sacraments of the Catholic Church. In 1993, a Perpetual Adoration Chapel opened at our church and I signed up for a Holy Hour and would visit other times when my schedule would permit. This was the best decision I have ever made and I encourage everyone to *find the time.*

Soon after DJ's birth into Eternal Life, while at Mass, I heard the beginning of Saint Paul's Letter to the Philippians which reminded me of one of DJ's letter so I went home and read the Letter. I then remembered it was the same Letter that the Lord gave me for DJ's fourth grade religion class,

"Shine on the world like bright stars"(Phil 2:15)

IMPORTANT NOTE: The definition of a star's light defined by Michigan State University Science Theater:

"The energy released in the star's center makes its way to the surface, where it is radiated into space as light ..."

To look at this from a Christian point of view: God should be our center so His Light shines through us to our world. Now let's listen to Saint Clare's words from Divine Office, August 11:

"...ponder His unspeakable Love which caused Him to suffer on the wood of the Cross...He said,'...is any sorrow like Mine.' Let us answer His cries and lamentations with one voice and one spirit: 'I will be mindful and remember and my soul will be consumed within me.' In this way... your love will burn with an ever brighter flame."

Now that's a star!

Since I do not believe in coincidences I saw this as a gift from DJ to help me live up to the advice he wrote at the end of his letter,

"Be strong. It'll all work out in the end."

My two children's birth into Eternal Life have left me a lasting legacy. DJ, October 13th which I have shared and the miscarriage of my ninth baby, Katrina Marie, June 6, 1987 the day Pope John Paul II declared "The **Year of Mary.**" To commemorated it he hosted a live television telecast to five continents in praying the rosary. It was estimated that the Pope led over one billion viewers in five different languages uniting God's people in this Global Prayer for Peace. Not only were the lives of my children a blessing, but through their births into Eternal Life, God allowed them to leave me a lasting blessing.

"Pray the Rosary."

"The wolf shall dwell with the lamb, and the leopard shall lie down with the kid, and the calf and the lion and the fatling together, <u>and a little child will lead them.</u> The cow and the bear shall feed; their young shall lie down together; and the lion shall eat straw like an ox. The suckling child shall play over the hole of the asp, and the weaned child shall put his hand on the adder's den. They shall not hurt or destroy in all My holy mountain; for the earth shall be full of the knowledge of the Lord as the waters cover the sea"(Is 11:6-9).

From DJ's birth into Eternal Life, the still, small Voice held me to speak only "The Truth." It amazed me how many people I knew were afraid of the Truth. They preferred things to remain hidden. But as a human being I have a right to live in dignity – the origin of this comes from the fact I am born in the likeness and image of God. In His wisdom He also wrote a natural law on our hearts to help us know right from wrong, good from evil, lie from Truth. I would no longer ignore my conscious or compromise the Truth. With God's Word to sustain me, the *"black hole"*, predicted from my own mouth, got blacker and after months and years of fighting for the Truth, I finally surrendered it all to God.

"Surrender to God, and He will do everything for you"(Ps 37:40).

And once I did, God reminded me I can only be responsible for what I do. So I continue to draw strength from the Sacraments of The Catholic Church as I keep my eyes on the Son, Jesus Christ *(like DJ's sunrise and sunset pictures!)*.

I also look at the example the Warrior Saint Michael the Archangel set, one of humble, loving prayer, and Blessed Mary's demand for us to *"Pray, pray, pray."* as Their Mission is one of Peace and to bring us to Her Son, Jesus Christ, our Lord and Savior.

TO JESUS THROUGH MARY.

With saving souls as my life's Mission I have committed my life to one of prayer through mortification.

"Commit your life to the Lord, Trust in Him and He will act" (Ps:37:5).

The connection to the military, due to the gift of being a Mom to now six sons in the United States Army, there is no turning back. I make the intent of this book to **unite the voices** of

*THE MEN AND WOMEN ON THE FRONT-LINES
to
*THOSE OF US ON THE HOME-FRONT
to
*THOSE WHO ARE FOREVER VIGILANT SOLDIERS IN HEAVEN

WITH AN INFANTRYMAN'S BATTLE CRY:

"NEVER QUIT, NEVER STOP!"

"You will suffer in the world, but have confidence: I have overcome the world"(John 16:33).